Pilgrims of the Alley

Living Out Faith in Displacement

DAVE ARNOLD

Urban Loft Publishers :: Portland, Oregon

Pilgrims of the Alley
Living Out Faith in Displacement

Urban Loft Publishers
2034 NE 40th Avenue #414
Portland, OR 97212
www.theurbanloft.org

ISBN:978-1482070101

Made in the U.S.A.

All Scripture quotations, unless otherwise indicated, are taken from the Holy Bible, NEW INTERNATIONAL VERSION®. Copyright © 1973, 1978, 1984, 2011 by Biblica, Inc. All rights reserved worldwide. Used by permission.

Cover design: Carl Johnson
Interior Design: Carl Johnson
www.saint-creative.com

Contents

To my wife, my co-laborer and closest companion in the alleys of life, and to my son, Luke – my little warrior who has a huge heart for God.

Foreword

This book inspires hope.

One warm summer evening, I climbed into a white rattley 15-passenger van to ride along with Dave Arnold to pick up a family of refugees arriving at Chicago's O'Hare International Airport. They had been forced to live in refugee camps in Southeast Asia because no country wanted them. But now they had the hope of a new beginning in America.

The family got off the plane wearing their immigration documents around their necks and carrying everything they owned in makeshift suitcases. They were afraid, tired, disoriented, and not able to speak a word of English. Through my tears I watched as Dave embraced this family with warmth, love, acceptance, and friendship.

Later, when we arrived at their new apartment Dave patiently taught them how to use a hot- and cold-water faucet, how to turn on and off the lights, how to use the stove and oven, and how to use a door key – because all these things were new to them.

At other times I accompanied Dave on follow-up visits to the homes of refugees, and saw how they would light up when he walked into their apartment because to them, Dave had become the face of hope.

The truths that you hold in your hands are not the result of academic research or a sociological think-tank; rather they flow from the family of Dave, Angie, and Luke Arnold who years ago decided to not only proclaim the good news of Jesus in words, but that they would, like Jesus, live among the displaced people of the world to embody the hope of the kingdom of God.

Hopelessness surrounds us. It's everywhere, whether among the refugees fleeing the war-torn regions of the world or in the self-destruction and violence found in our own neighborhoods. Even the children of God who should be offering hope to the world have themselves become hopeless because of their feelings of inadequacy.

Pilgrims of the Alley uses creative approaches to guide the children of God into a better understanding of our own pilgrimages, and to realize that our feelings of displacement from this world can actually provide for us the means of reaching out and connecting to others.

It has been said that we are never more like God than when we offer hope to others. It is my prayer that the hope illustrated in Dave's book will not only draw you into the future with a renewed enthusiasm, but it will also give you the practical means to move those who are displaced to a place of belonging.

May the God of hope fill you with all joy and peace as you trust in him, so that you may overflow with hope by the power of the Holy Spirit. (Romans 15:13)

Lewie Clark is the President of Icon Ministries, and the author of *Imitating Jesus: Love, Friendship, and Disciple-Making.*

Chicago
January, 2013

What Others Are Saying

"Dave aptly slips on the shoes of the pilgrim and walks their journey through displacement. *Pilgrims of the Alley* will surprise, console, and encourage those already on the journey, and also those who choose to slip on pilgrim shoes to strengthen their own faith. It's personal, biblically-anchored, and absolutely inspirational. I highly recommend it." -- **Stephan J. Bauman**, President & CEO, World Relief

"*Pilgrims of the Alley* gives me hope of things to come. Dave writes with a profound purpose and reflects the light of a loving God calling his people home." -- **Justin Zoradi**, Founder of These Numbers Have Faces and JustinZoradi.com

"I was reminded and encouraged that living out our love for Christ as aliens in this land is essential for an authentic and vibrant faith in our broken world." -- **Noel Castellanos**, CEO, Christian Community Development Association

"You're looking at a book that will move you to feel compassion and motivate you to express the love of God to your corner of the world. Dave Arnold has done an exceptional job of merging personal experience, story, and biblical guidance into the message of this book. It is a message easy to read and hard to forget." -- **Tim Grissom**, Best-selling author (co-author of *Seeking Him: Experiencing the Joy of Personal Revival*) and editor

"Dave Arnold has a sensitivity seen in few writers today. His heart is transparent in his words. His message is contemporary, but its value is timeless. Younger readers will value the teaching of this book, but readers of all ages will see themes they can identify with, learn from, and desire to pass on." -- **Dr. Dennis E. Hensley**, Author of *The Power of Positive Productivity* and Professor of Professional Writing, Taylor University

"Dave Arnold has long championed the cause of refugees and now offers fresh thoughts on our own sense of displacement as exiles and pilgrims in this world. Yet he reminds us that God is at work in our displacement and is preparing His people for permanent residency one day with Him. Thanks Dave, for modeling a heart for the stranger and challenging us to a similar investment of our lives." -- **Dr. John Fuder**, Director of Justice & Compassion Ministries, Resource Global/Heart for the City, Chicago

"This book took my attention from the beginning and brought back memories for me. Having spent a couple of years living in a camp, as a refugee, myself, I found myself in each of the three stages of displacement that Dave Arnold describes. This made me wonder, 'How does this man know all this about me without having met me?' As I continued reading this book, I learned many things about myself as well. I recommend this book as a good resource for people in ministry. If you read and understand this book, you are half-way to impacting new immigrants for the Kingdom of God." -- **Muhammad al Hallaaj**, Salaam Ministries, Edmonton, Canada, Author of *More Than a Dream*

"From his time on my staff at NorthRidge, I know Dave to be an authentic, thoughtful, and committed Christ follower. His ministry to the poor and displaced of our world has uniquely qualified him to write this book. It will encourage you, make you think, and challenge you to action." -- **Brad Powell**, Senior Pastor of NorthRidge Church and author of *Change Your Church for Good*

"*Pilgrims of the Alley* is a dangerous book. I picked it up to skim through the book and couldn't put it down. The story captures your attention and it inspires you. This book really opened my eyes and I know I'll never be the same - but that's a good thing. I highly suggest you not only buy a copy for yourself but buy one for a friend, it's that good! We don't have to live in defeat anymore. Thanks for the reminder Dave!" -- **Kimanzi Constable**, Author of *Are You Living or Existing*, International Speaker and Consultant.

"I love what Dave has done with this book. In his words: 'This book is about a journey of understanding how to navigate a life of faith amid a world of such uncertainty, of darkness, and oftentimes, of great despair.' I'm a firm believer that our faith grows in unexpected places. In his book, Dave writes passionately from the heart. He has lived and experienced brokenness in displacement. This book will call you to abandon yourself to a purpose bigger than life itself. This is about the God-intended life - pouring ourselves into others so we can live the life that matter. Get a copy of this book!" -- **Joseph Iregbu**, Writer, Speaker, Leadership Coach and Author of *SELAH: A 90-Day Journey of Grace and Hope*

"If you are interested in a story about a personal, passionate encounter with God, this is a must-read. I was inspired and moved by the simplicity yet authenticity of Dave's insight on God's work in our daily lives. I was specifically touched by his ability to unlock God's purpose behind being the 'Alley.' You will learn that the Alley is a necessary part of the journey, and you will probably be encouraged to walk through it. And when you do, you'll know there's hope, hope in the Alley – for everyone walking through it." -- **Lilian Samaan**, Executive Director, World Relief Chicago

"It was with much anticipation that I eagerly read *Pilgrims in the Alley* by my friend and co-laborer in the Lord, Dave Arnold. With a poetic and lyrical style that weaves biblical narrative and personal experience the reader is challenged to follow Jesus into displacement. This is not the writing of someone living and working among the urban immigrant just to 'pimp' their experience, but the expression of authentic fellow pilgrims. Read the book, reflect on its message and live it." -- **Clive Craigen**, Assistant Professor Urban Ministry, Director of the Urban Cohort Program, Moody Bible Institute

"A rare book that takes us beyond dry theories and reveals behind-the-scenes, real-life stories of working with broken and displaced peoples. An essential and comprehensive work that poignantly reminds us that we who belong to Christ will always feel as displaced in this world, as those refugees Arnold has worked with throughout his life and career.

As Arnold points out, it's normal that we feel uneasy and uncomfortable in this world: this is not our home." -- **Matt Brown**, Evangelist, Author and Founder of Think Eternity

"Dave Arnold is the real deal, and models the very self-sacrifice that he calls upon us as Christ followers to embrace. This book will expose you to a radical vision of hospitality, and will give you practical suggestions for how to move towards that reality." -- **Daniel Hill**, Senior Pastor, River City Community Church, Chicago, IL

Introduction

Displacement: *noun*
1. To move something from its natural environment
2. The act of uniform movement

It all began one gray morning in Chicago a number of years ago. I had recently started working with an organization that helps resettle refugees to Chicago by providing them with affordable housing, teaching them English, helping them find jobs, and other adjustment services. On this particular day, I was loading up the cargo van with donated furniture to be delivered to an apartment that would soon be the new home of a refugee family due to arrive shortly.

As I loaded the van in the back alley behind the office, I caught a movement from the corner of my eye. It was a grayish figure who appeared quite suddenly from around the corner and into the openness of the alley. He was an older man with a long beard and a pipe in his teeth. The smell of aromatic tobacco filled the air as he searched for something, his eyes darting back and forth as he scanned the alley.

"How's it going?" I said.

"Fine," he mumbled without looking up. He continued his search, frantically sifting through the large, green dumpster. A lady (perhaps his wife) came around the corner, dragging behind her a small suitcase, and joined him in his scavenging. She looked wearied and her shoulders slumped.

"Argh," the man said in a huff, slamming the dumpster lid down. He whipped out a lighter and quickly relit his pipe, scanning the horizon before him, his eyes locked on the other dumpsters that littered the alleyway. He must have been looking for something, but had obviously not found it in that dumpster. And so he moved on, with his lady lagging behind, and turned the corner down another alley. I waited a few minutes, and then out of curiosity slowly crept behind them.

The man went from dumpster to dumpster, opening and closing lids. *I wonder where they're going? What is he looking for?* I thought to myself. My guess was that this couple was homeless, and was looking for some thrown-out item that, to them, had value and could

11

better their lifestyle. For many on the streets, what others treat as garbage, they treat as treasure.

Displaced Persons

Observing these pilgrims in the alley, I began to think about God and the world we live in. I was unable to shake their image from my mind. As followers of Jesus, we too are homeless in this world, wandering about as strangers in a place that's not our own. We are the pilgrims of the alley, striving to live as citizens of another world while trying to make it in this one. We are made for heavenly mansions but are stuck in earthbound alleys.

Following World War II, 250,000 Jewish Holocaust survivors lived in refugee camps in Germany, Austria, and Italy.[1] They were called *displaced persons* or DPs.

These DPs were placed in camps so they could attempt to recover from all that they had suffered, heal, rebuild their lives, be in community with others, and begin the daunting process of locating family members that had also survived the Holocaust.

The attempt to reunite families went hand in hand with the creation of new ones; for there were many weddings and births in the DP camps.[2] Slowly, these survivors were able to rebuild their lives. Schools were started in the camps, Jewish holidays were reinstated, and eventually, the United States, Canada, Israel, and South Africa accepted these displaced people and gave them permanent residency.

Unfortunately the world hasn't changed much since then; wars, genocide, and persecution still persist. As a result, there are still millions of displaced persons who have either fled or been forcibly evicted from their homelands and live in unnatural, makeshift environments such as refugee camps or in bordering countries where they hide out from government or military authorities and learn to survive.

---

1 United State Holocaust Memorial Museum, "Displaced Persons."

2 Ibid.

Many of the refugees I work with long to return to their country of origin, but they cannot. All they have are memories: memories of what life was like before the darkness fell, and the hope that someday things will be normal again and they can return.

An Environment of Change

This book is about a journey of understanding how to navigate a life of faith amid a world of such uncertainty, of darkness, and oftentimes, of great despair. The fact is, as followers of Jesus, we are displaced persons. To be displaced means to be away from or out of one's natural environment. And I believe it's in this environment our faith grows the most.

Why? Because God is at work in displacement.

In the following chapters, I hope to uncover some truths of how God takes ordinary people like you and me and places us in environments that challenge and forge us into extraordinary people.

I hope to convince you that extraordinary growth takes place in the alleys of life – in an unnatural and oftentimes hostile environment – and not by attempting to fit into this world through status or image or even Christian duty. You will also meet some extraordinary pilgrims, men and woman who have remarkable stories to tell of how they live out their faith as displaced persons.

Recapturing the Memory

The Scripture passage this book is based on comes from the famous discourse we know as the Last Supper. It is, I believe, a timeless narrative that points both to our present-day realities while shedding light on our fears and that gnawing ache that grows within.

In one of the darkest nights the world has ever known, a night which would change the whole course of history, Jesus began to prepare His disciples for His departure.

"Do not let your hearts be troubled. Trust in God; trust also in me. In my Father's house are many rooms; if it were not so, I would have told you. I am going to prepare a place for you. And if I go and prepare a place for you, I will come back and take you to be with me that you also may be where I am. You know the way to the place where I am going" (John 14:1-4).

These words, I believe, marked the beginning of a great human journey – from despair and uncertainty to hope and longing. Because the truth is many of us have lost our way. So when Thomas immediately asks Jesus, "Lord, we don't know where you are going, so how can we know the way?" (14:4), His reply answered not only Thomas' question, He answered ours as well.

I am the way, and the truth, and the life ...

Madeleine L' Engle wrote, "One of the great sorrows which came to human beings when Adam and Eve left the Garden was the loss of memory, memory of all that God's children are meant to be."[3] I hope to recapture a bit of that memory, a memory buried beneath the daunting realities of the world we live in.

Sadly there are many who have fallen into despair and hopelessness and cannot seem to remember anything good, let alone hope for something better to come. But all is not lost. God wants to change us into amazing, courageous, loving, hopeful people. He wants to do impossible things through us.

He wants us to mature and grow and learn to see through the thick fog of the world and peer into Heaven's delights. He wants us to remember all that we've forgotten and to long for all that await us.

It's not easy to be displaced, to live in an environment that is unnatural. But it is possible to find great joy and hope and restoration in the midst of it. Just as the Jewish Holocaust survivors did.

We can learn (by God's grace) to be the right kind of people – the people of God and His love – in displacement while we wait for Christ to come back and give us placement and permanent residency.

So I invite you to join me on this pilgrimage and adventure that I myself am on. My adventure began on that gray morning in Chicago. And as G.K. Chesterton reminds us, "adventures happen on dull days, and not on sunny ones. When the chord of monotony is stretched most tight, then it breaks with a sound like a song."[4]

---

3 L'Engle, *Walking on Water*, 11.

4 Chesterton, *Napoleon of Notting Hill*, 11.

After a few minutes on that day, the old man with the pipe and his lady turned down another alley never to be seen by me again. But their memory stayed with me. So let's follow them through the alleys of life and try to recapture the memory of all that God has meant us to be.

DISORIENTATION

SECTION ONE

Chapter 1

ACHE: The Story We Find Ourselves In

"We are designed to enjoy a better world than this. And until that better world comes along, we will groan for what we do not have. An aching soul is evidence not of neurosis or spiritual immaturity, but of realism." (Larry Crabb)

Disorientation: *noun*
1. Confusion (usually transient) about where you are and how to proceed.

Once on the TV news program *60 Minutes*, I heard a businessman from San Francisco describe his work ethic. This particular edition highlighted CEOs who were very successful in spite of our nation's economic struggles. This particular CEO said the secret to his success was to work all the time. He told the reporter that he never takes a break, not even in the shower, where he has a special waterproof phone, so he can make calls or be available if a call comes in. The reporter asked, "So what happens if you don't work?"

"I ache," he said.

I thought about that for some time. Why do we ache? I mean, aren't we supposed to be happy and fulfilled and prosperous – especially as Christians?

For years I too attempted to push away my ache through working, attempting to find my identity and significance through what I did, or what people expected of me, or what I thought God expected of me. After all, I worked for the Lord. At least that's what I told myself.

I've heard some preachers say that to struggle or have doubts about our walk with God means we lack faith; we don't pray and read the Bible enough. I once heard a preacher justify the fact he was a workaholic by saying, "I'd rather burn out on God than burn out on anything else."

But no matter how much we do for God, how many people we seek to please, or how busy we are, the ache remains – a feeling that something is not right in our world, or more substantially, something's not right in us. It's the story we find ourselves in.

The Three Stages of Displacement

For the last eight years or so, I've worked with refugees from all over the world. I see three main stages a refugee typically goes through. The first is *disorientation*.

When a new refugee arrives, he or she is often overwhelmed with the daunting task of learning a new language, adapting to a new culture, trying to find a job and good schools for the children, and so on.

The second is *assimilation* – or, what I call *blessing*. This is where refugees learn to assimilate into their new environment. They're more "at home." They have jobs, can speak the language, and are deeply grateful to be in a new land. But most importantly they desire to give back. That is, they no longer want a hand up (relying on welfare or other government services) but desire to be citizens of America and contribute.

The third stage is homecoming. There comes a time when the refugee longs to return back to their homeland. Most refugees I know have learned to love America. Many of them work very hard – sometimes at more than one job – so their kids can go off to college or so they can buy a home one day. But that doesn't override their intense desire to go back to their place of origin. Many of them, however, cannot go back because of war or safety issues. But they hold on to the hope that one day things will be better.

I suggest these are the same stages we must go through as well. If we want to be "successful" in our faith-adventure here on earth and live meaningful and purposeful lives in displacement, it's vital to understand each of these stages.

This book, therefore, is organized under the three stages just mentioned:

1. *Disorientation:* As displaced persons, we find ourselves disoriented. To be disoriented means to be uncertain and

confused on how to move forward. This is the place where God wants us to be, because it's also the place of His presence.

1. *Blessing:* As we learn to rely on God's presence in our disoriented state, we come to see our purpose: namely, to bless others, especially the vulnerable and poor and hurting. This is the place where God teaches us to love.

2. *Homecoming:* Our final stage is longing. As we face our disorientation by relying on God's presence, and we embrace our purpose through loving and blessing others, we keep going, refusing to be pushed off course, because we know we are meant for a much better world than this.

It is in displacement, I suggest, where God is most active – as Jesus' disciples also discovered.

Passover

The air was brisk, typical of a March evening in Jerusalem. It blew in from the east, rolling over the hills and into the upper room. The atmosphere was solemn, almost eerily quiet. Peter glanced outside; he could hear sounds of laughter and celebration in the distance. It was one of the most important nights of the year – the night of the Passover Meal.

But this Passover felt different. The Rabbi did something unexpected, turning the festive meal – as they would soon discover – into a moment that would change history. By now, the disciples were used to Jesus' surprises. But this was something unexpected.

It started off in the old familiar way. The disciples were feasting to their hearts' delight. The aroma of fresh, unleavened bread wafted through the air. There was wine, figs, honey, olive oil, garlic, lamb... you name it. They leaned with their left arms on plush couch-cushions, and with their right hands, ate from the three tables that were enclosed by the couches. It was more than a meal, it was an eating experience!

The mood shifted rapidly, however, when the Rabbi got up, went behind the couches, took off His outer garment, got a pitcher of water, and washed the feet of His men. The disciples, still in the reclining position, with bread and wine to their lips, were speechless, immovable. *This is no posture for a Rabbi*, thought James. *What is He doing?* groaned Peter. *Only slaves do this*, John muttered. But no one spoke.

When Jesus came to Peter, Peter broke the silence and said, "No! You shall never wash my feet!"

Jesus answered, looking deeply into his eyes, "Unless I wash you, you have no part with Me."

"Then wash all of me, Lord, not just my feet," Peter said humbly.

"Do you know what I have done for you?" Jesus asked them. Their eyes darted back and forth, wondering who would speak. Judas, especially, seemed nervous; he had been acting strange all night. "I have set for you an example," Jesus continued. "You should serve one another as I have served you; for no servant is greater than his master."

The Rabbi went on, the mood growing heavier as He talked about how one of them would betray Him, and that He would soon leave them. Talk about disoriented! They forgot all about the feast. Everyone had lost their appetite.

As Jesus continued, urging them to learn to love one another, He said, "I have to leave to go prepare a place for you, but I will come again and receive you to Myself, that where I am, there you may be also. And you know the way where I am going."

The disciples were shocked. *He's leaving us? He's going to prepare a place for us? What does he mean?* Thomas was the first one to speak. "Lord, we do not know where You are going; so how do we know the way?"

When Life Doesn't Work

I believe this is the story we find ourselves in, the narrative we live by, found in John 13 through 17. The disciples are not as removed from us as we think. They became disillusioned. They lost hope. They despaired. They were displaced. What happened in the next few hours bears this out: Judas betrays Jesus with a kiss, which leads to His arrest; Peter attempts to control the situation by lashing out with a sword; and the disciples disappear, as their hopes in their beloved Rabbi – the

Messiah they thought would deliver Israel from her foes – came crashing down.

Simply put, life didn't work out for them as they thought. And life often doesn't work out the way we think it should, either.

I suggest, then, we find ourselves in similar stories. The disciples grew alarmed and disoriented in the upper room that night – and in our lives too, a sudden change of circumstance can often create a similar response. The vacation of our dreams turns sour. The much-needed romantic evening ends in arguments and silence. The loss of a job cracks our family's foundation. A disease is discovered. Bills pile up. The government and politicians promise a better life and stability, but to no avail.

"The whole creation groans," Paul says (Romans 8:22).[1] That includes us. During the Last Supper, Jesus told his anxious disciples, "Do not let your hearts be troubled" (John 14:27). And yet, though we are called to have faith, to not lean on our own understanding, and to find refuge under the protective wings of God's love, if we are honest with ourselves, we'll admit our hearts are indeed troubled.

East of Eden

During the Last Supper discourse, Jesus attempted to make it clear to the disciples that He is the One who makes life work, that He is the Promised Seed of Genesis 3:15. Although the snake (Satan) would first strike His heel to try to kill Him (the crucifixion), Jesus would ultimately prevail and would crush the head of His enemy (the resurrection).

When a snake's head is crushed, its central nervous system takes over and its body writhes usually for a few hours until the snake eventually dies.

At the crucifixion and resurrection of Christ, Satan's head was crushed. He was dealt a death blow. But his body (his influence) is still to this day violently reacting. Satan knows his time is short, and so he's doing everything he can to make a mess of things. Because of this,

---

1 NASB.

23

while we wait for the return of Christ, our hearts will be troubled because the enemy is doing everything he can to poison this world.

Jesus warned His disciples about this, telling them of dark times ahead. The disciples didn't get it, and oftentimes we don't either. And so we set out on this quest through the alleys of life, aching for everything to be whole and right. But it's beyond our reach.

So the ache remains. Indeed it must remain. If we got the instant relief we crave and all of our longings and desires in our sojourn through life were satisfied, would we really seek after Christ? Would we really need Him at all? The simple fact is that just like Adam and Eve, when God kicked them out of the Garden, we too live east of Eden.

What we long for, what we are made for, lies in the future. Some days the visibility is clear; we can see for miles, and we sense our destination is close at hand. But most of the time we're disoriented – in a fog of confusion about where we are and where we are headed.

In the meantime, our quest is for what Jesus promised His disciples in the upper room: His presence. Yes, Jesus had to leave them, but in His place He promised to send the Holy Spirit, the Counselor who comforts and strengthens us as we wait for His return (John 14:26-28).

God's presence is the lamp we hold, in whose light the darkness of the alley is overcome. It's the story we find ourselves in.

Reflections From the Alley

1. When life doesn't work out the way you hoped, how do you respond?

2. Read John 13 through 17. What do you think Jesus' main message was to His disciples? How does this message apply to you?

Lord Jesus, I thank you for Your promises. I know You had to go and prepare a place for me, and will one day come back to take me with You there. In the meantime, I struggle in this world full of darkness and uncertainties. Help me, Lord, to trust in You for my life's meaning and purpose. Please protect me from the enemy and his schemes. Guide me, I pray, according to Your plan and lead me safely home to where You are. In Jesus' name, Amen.

Chapter 2

ORPHANED: *The Ache Made Manifest*

"So long as God's will runs parallel to ours, we follow blithely. But the moment that they cross, or clash, that life grows difficult, that we don't understand, how apt faith is to fail us just when we have most need of it!" (A.J. Gossip)

Years ago I led a college ministry at a large church. It was while ministering to college students that I realized something both within myself and within others: the need to belong. Belonging is a powerful word; it is crucial if we are to understand the story we live in and our culture around us.

There was a certain young man who came to the ministry, desperately looking to belong. I'll call him Steve. Steve had a rough past and battled with mental and emotional issues. I remember the night he walked into our service. Like a stray dog wounded by its master, he cowered in the back of the room, avoiding eye contact and communication. When we had group discussions, Steve remained in the back.

At the end of the service, I made it a point to introduce myself to Steve and to others in the group. Although he was friendly and seemed happy to meet people, he was also nervous and kept his distance.

Reluctantly he came out to dinner with us. After a few weeks, he became a regular in the group. One particular evening, Steve, who still stayed in the back, surprised me by saying, "Nobody cares for me. Everyone hates me."

"What?" I said in reply. "Steve, that's not true. We care about you."

"Maybe you do," he said, "but nobody else does. Everyone hates me."

"That's not true," I told him again. And it wasn't, at least from my perspective. I thought the group did an incredible job at welcoming Steve. They always invited him to dinner afterward. A few people even got his phone number so they could hang out with him.

In spite of this, Steve really didn't believe people cared about him. As I learned more about him and his family of origin and upbringing, I could see where this came from – from a deep place inside, a place he was still trapped in due to unmet childhood needs.

The Importance of Belonging

The truth is, all of us feel this way at certain times. We feel alone and dejected, as if nobody notices us or would even care if we disappeared. Although this may not be true in reality, it is true internally. Much of this is due to our culture, which prizes itself on autonomy and individualism.

But even more troubling is the fact that like Steve, many of us did not get our emotional needs met as children. And one of those needs is to belong.

Belonging is crucial to our self-worth, emotional security, and a sense of significance. Joseph Hellerman, in his book, *When the Church Was a Family: Recapturing Jesus' Vision for Authentic Christian Community*, writes, "We turn to psychologists – and to medication – to assist us in dealing with the stress and emotional upheaval that inevitably come on us in a society that emphasizes self-reliance and individual autonomy at the expense of relational support and accountability... In other words, the great majority of people on this planet never needed therapy until society began to dump the responsibility for making life's major decisions squarely upon the lonely shoulders of the individual."[1]

The Bible says we reap what we sow (Galatians 6:7), and we have sown to individuality for a long time. It's no surprise we wonder why we feel so alone, so isolated. The Fall put enmity between us and God, and between us and others. Adam blamed Eve, who blamed the serpent.

---

1 Hellerman, *When the Church Was a Family*, 29.

Detached

Think about it: we often detach people from caring communities, in order for them to get fixed so they can function back in community. We rely on professionals to help make us "normal" again so we can live without all the discomforts and problems that are inevitable in a fallen world.

This was the situation with Steve. He was in special needs groups most of his life – learning disability programs, special needs sports programs, and so on – but what we had, as a spiritual community, was what he longed for, a group of people who loved him and accepted him as he was. I think he tasted it, but his fear caused him to withdraw and believe the lie that he is different and therefore not special.

Because of the culture we live in, many of us feel detached and disoriented. So what are we to do? I don't think there are any quick-fix solutions or multi-step programs. But I do think there are a couple of truths we can hold on to.

Truth Number One: Presence

Jesus told His disciples in the upper room, "I will not leave you as orphans; I will come to you" (John 14:18).[2]

In the Roman Empire during the time of Christ, when a baby was born, the father of the family, or the oldest living male, known as the *paterfamilias*, had the power to decide whether or not to keep the newborn. Once the child was delivered, the midwife placed the baby on the floor to see what the father would do. If he picked the baby up, he or she was accepted and brought into his home. If he did not, because he determined the baby to be deformed in some way, or because he had too many children already, the baby would be taken out of the home and abandoned. The universal assumption was the baby would be picked up by someone else and taken in as a slave.[3]

---

2 NASB.

3 Public Broadcasting Service, "The Roman Empire in the First Century: Family Life."

Jesus possibly drew from this imagery when He lovingly tells His "babies" they will not be orphaned, left out in the street to be picked up to live as slaves. On the contrary, they belong forever to Jesus, to His Father, to the Spirit, and to the Kingdom.

We too belong. Perhaps in your family you never felt you fit in. Your sister or brother was the favorite or special sibling. Perhaps you were told, whether intentionally or unintentionally, you were an "accident" – mom and dad did not plan on having you.

But you belong. You are not an accident, left out in the cold to fend for yourself. We must remember God's loving-kindness and faithfulness – the promise that He is with us always. Only His presence now, in our lives, can remedy the ache we feel.

> "But *you* belong. You are not an accident, left out in the cold to fend for yourself."

Truth Number Two: Togetherness

There is second truth we must hold to if we are to deal with our ache: our presence with others. Simply put, we cannot live in isolation. Jesus said, "For where two or three are gathered in My name, I am there in their midst" (Matthew 18:20).[4] Jesus' presence is with us when we are with each other.

Jesus showed His followers how to live when He was with them, and how to live when He was not. "A new command I give you: Love one another. As I have loved you, so you must love one another. By this all men will know that you are my disciples, if you love one another" (John 13:34-35). In other words, Jesus said, "You belong to Me and I have loved you; now show that you belong to each other by doing the same."

Hellerman says, "Jesus radically challenged His disciples to disavow primary loyalty to their natural families in order to join the new surrogate family of siblings He was establishing – the family of

---

4 NASB.

God."[5] Hellerman uses the phrase "strong group" to stress the fact that in the Mediterranean world of Jesus, people thought collectively, as a group, as opposed to we in the West who think more individualistically.

I have seen this working with refugees and immigrants. For the last seven years, I have worked primarily with folks from the Middle East (especially Iraq and Palestine), North Africa, and South Asia (Burma and Nepal). All of them come from a strong group culture. They think in terms of their families or tribes, not as individuals. They eat together as families. They make decisions based on what is good for the group. They support each other financially, often sending money to their families back home.

When I lived in Chicago there was a man in my neighborhood who was Palestinian. His job was to sell socks. All day, rain or shine (or snow – it's Chicago after all!) he would stand on the sidewalk and call out, "Socks, socks, socks," as people walked by.

On a good day, he made thirty dollars, which was enough money for him to send some back to his wife and children in the West Bank. The money he made, although minimal by American standards, provided his family with enough food for survival. His sacrifice – being away from them – was worth doing for the betterment of his family.

Many people throughout the world think naturally about belonging to each other. Sadly, we in the West lean toward independence and separation from one another. We tend to make major life-decisions, such as who to marry, where to live, where to work, based on our own wants and interests rather than through the supportive advice of others.

Christian fellowship has to be more than a once-a-week event. It's not a formula or a three-step quick fix. It's relational and holistic, where we learn to live in God's presence and within community.

If we are going to face our ache, we must face it with others. We need to be present in people's lives, and have them present in our lives. Going to a church service on Sunday morning and shaking a few hands doesn't cut it. We need brothers and sisters in Christ, people who you know will be present in your life – people you know and who know you.

---

5 *When the Church Was a Family*, 64.

31

You're Not Alone

Isolation is one of the principal daggers the enemy throws at us in this world. He knows if he can make us feel desperate to the point that we question God's presence in our lives or in this world, then he can really do some damage. But he goes further. Satan will try not only to turn you from God and tempt you to deal with your ache without Him, but to turn you away from others, by making us think that "nobody understands me" or "I might as well face the fact I'm alone."

You are not alone! God is with you. Other people, the right people, caring, compassionate, selfless people, can also be there, too. We all ache. That's inevitable. The question is, do we ache alone or not?

Reflections from the Alley

1. Why do you think belonging is so important?

2. What kind of community do you have around you? Is it the right kind of community, the kind that helps you to be more of the person God wants you to be?

Lord, I thank You for Your presence in my life. I confess how often I try to live independently from you, thinking I know what is best for my life. I don't. I need You to walk with me, to guide me. I also pray that You would help me to be in the right kind of community, a community of people who care and love. Help me to not succumb to the lie that I don't need others. In Jesus' name I pray, Amen.

Chapter 3

PRESENCE: God in the Kitchen

"Lord of pots and pans and things ...
Make me a saint by getting meals
And washing up the plates!"
(Ancient Prayer)

When most people think about God and where He can be found, they think of a cathedral, a church building, stained glass, pews, the mountains, the ocean, a desert, or up in the sky somewhere.

But what about everyday, ordinary places like ... the kitchen? Can God be there? Or can God be found in the city? In the alley? Having dinner with a Muslim family? At a brothel in Amsterdam? It is sad to think that much of our Christian thinking in the last thirty years or so has been a Christianity as defined by the suburbs, the countryside, and church buildings.

We often see Hallmark cards depicting Bible verses with mountains, lush meadows, or a majestic sea in the background. I don't think I've ever seen a card with a Bible verse and a city in the background. Is God only at work in meadows and mountains? Does He only show up during church services?

A Lowly Brother

Long ago there was a guy who lived in Paris in a time where many were questioning spiritual things, when skepticism flourished, and the Enlightenment age, like a dark shadow, hovered over the European landscape. It was a time of questioning and progressive thinking. It was during this era that the philosopher, René Descartes, coined his famous saying, "I think, therefore I am."

During the Enlightenment, the focus turned from the I AM (the belief in and reverence for God) to the "I am" (the self, self-awareness, and humanism). Francis Schaeffer stated this well when he wrote,

"Humanism in the larger, more inclusive sense, is the system whereby men and women, beginning absolutely by themselves, try rationally to build out from themselves, having only Man as their integration point, to find all knowledge, meaning and value."[1]

But in the midst of this, a man by the name of Brother Lawrence lived tucked away in a Carmelite monastery in the heart of Paris. Although Paris was abuzz with the allure of reason and questioning, Brother Lawrence spent his days in the kitchen serving others and falling in love with his God.[2]

In the dead of winter, eighteen-year-old Nicholas Herman had an encounter with a tree. That's right, a tree.

Young Nicholas stumbled upon a dead tree, completely leafless, weighed down with snow and bruised by ice. As he observed this tree, he was gripped by the thought of his own dead, lifeless soul. He realized, at that moment, he was just like that tree. God spoke to him and revealed to him His love, majesty and romance – and he was changed.

At the age of thirty, he enrolled in a life of prayer and solitude as a monk with the Carmelite Order in Paris. It was at this monastery that Nicholas received his new name – Brother Lawrence.

Unfortunately for this new brother, his lofty hope of meditation, solitude and prayer came to an abrupt halt when he was given the job of kitchen-duty for the monastery, cooking meals for forty fellow monks and cleaning up the slop from their plates. But it was in the kitchen that a radical transformation took place in Brother Lawrence.

His letters reflect this experience, an experience he called "the practice of the presence of God."

Sanctuary

Rather than grow bitter and disillusioned with his job, Lawrence accepted it and thanked God for it. The kitchen became his personal sanctuary. "'The time of business,' said he, 'does not with me differ

---

1 Schaeffer, *Trilogy,* 9.

2 Thanks for the helpful insight into the life of Brother Lawrence by Steve Case, author of *God is Here: Connecting with Him in Everyday Life.*

from the time of prayer; and in the kitchen, while several persons are at the same time calling for different things, I possess God in as great tranquility as if I were upon my knees at the blessed sacrament.'"[3]

Lawrence was so filled with God's love and joy that many in Paris and all of France came to learn this simple man's secret. The Bishop of France, in fact, came to meet this humble brother.

Although Lawrence did other jobs too, such as stocking up on the wine and working in the shoe shop fixing sandals, the kitchen was his Mount Sinai – the place where he first sought the face of God. "For more than fifty years," Case writes, "Brother Lawrence prayed and conversed and shared his ideas on the practice of the presence of God."[4]

The Kitchen

It's interesting to think of the kitchen as a spiritual place, or a place of personal growth. In literature, the kitchen is symbolic of a place of healing, redemption and growth. In the Grimm Brothers' fairytale, *Iron John*, the main character (an eight-year-old prince with golden hair), goes on an adventure with a Wild Man.

The Wild Man mentors the young prince, leading him from boyhood to manhood. *Iron John* is a story of masculinity and the stages a boy goes through to become a man.

Part of this process involves the boy going to live in a castle obscurely to learn humility. Rather than moving up the ranks of the nobility, the boy descends downward to work in the dark, dingy basement of the castle where the kitchen was located. There, the boy carries wood and buckets of water and learns to cook.

In his poignant rendition of this classic tale, Robert Bly says this regarding the kitchen: "To fall from being a king's son to being a cook is the step the story asks for. Carrying wood and water, working in the basement of the castle – where the kitchen is – stands for the Drop Through the Floor, the Descent, the humiliation, the 'way down and

---

3 Brother Lawrence, *The Practice of the Presence of God with Spiritual Maxims.*

4 *God is Here,* 9.

out'... The mark of Descent, whether undertaken consciously or unconsciously, is a newly arrived-at lowliness, associated with water and soul, as height is associated with spirit. 'Water prefers low places.'"[5]

We also see this portrayed in *Cinderella*, where the young peasant-turned-princess is scrubbing the kitchen floor of her wicked stepmother's house.

The kitchen is often deemed as a place that is lowly, where one serves without any attention or applause; a place of peasants and paupers, not the wealthy elites.

I think I have an inside glimpse of this lifestyle. I married a chef who spends more of her time in the kitchen than anywhere else. Although Angie does not work at a restaurant, she is a master chef, nevertheless. She is Sicilian/Italian and cooking is in her blood.

Ever since she was a little girl she has been experimenting with cooking and baking. Honestly (and I am not just saying this because I am her husband) she is an incredible cook. Everyone she cooks for says so.

I consider her to be my own up-close-and-personal "Sister Lawrence" because her sanctuary is her kitchen. It is here, amid cooking and baking and creating, that she connects with God and worships Him.

On any given day, I experience the intoxicating smells of fresh cookies, her famous banana bread, home-made pasta sauce (the best!), freshly brewed coffee, and on it goes. In our home, the kitchen is the center where everything comes together.

I have learned from Angie that cooking is an art. It takes discipline, time, and precision. Cooking is not throwing leftovers in the microwave or breaking out frozen meals – anyone can do that.

It's something to work at, perfect, experiment. My wife is the Picasso-in-the-kitchen, fashioning and shaping amazing and scrumptious creations.

---

5 Bly, *Iron John*, 69.

Ordinary Places

Brother Lawrence understood that the kingdom of God can be expressed anywhere, no matter how menial the task or how small the feat. The traditional places we often think of concerning God's work are not the only places where God shows up.

Really, I wonder if He shows up more often in the least expected and ordinary places of our lives.

God is at work in the kitchen, as you wash dishes after a dinner with friends. He is at work in the middle of the night when your child is sick. He is at work when you decide it would be better to take a walk and enjoy nature rather than eat lunch at your desk.

God is at work all around us. We just have to have the eyes to see it. Not only will He not leave us as orphans, He promises to show up in every part of our lives, whether we're aware of it or not. Our job as pilgrims is to learn to see it – the unexpected manifestation of God in the ordinary.

Reflections from the Alley

1. In what unexpected places have you experienced God?

2. Have you ever found yourself in the "kitchen," in a low place or circumstance? What lessons did you learn?

Lord, thank You for working in the unexpected places of my life. Help me to see You throughout the day, to hear Your voice, and to know You are with me. Thank You that I am not left alone to fend for myself in this world. Help me to see where You are working so I can join You. Even in our lowest times, Your presence is with me. I recognize I can do nothing without You. Thank You for being with me always, in Jesus' name, Amen.

Chapter 4

PENNIES: God's Reminders to Keep Going

"The question is, not what you look at, but what you see."
(Henry David Thoreau)

My wife, Angie, started a unique habit many years ago when we first moved to Chicago. Everywhere we'd go in that vast, urban jungle, she'd find a penny. To this day, she still finds them.

She finds them on the streets, in city parks, on sidewalks, inside stores, and just about any place you could possibly think of. Inevitably, we'll be out taking a stroll with our son, on a date, or in deep conversation, and my wife stops cold turkey, bends down and says, "Look, I found one," and proceeds to dust off her newly found, tiny copper treasure. She's so excited, as if she just found a hundred dollar bill.

I know what you're thinking: "What's with the penny obsession?" I understand where you're coming from. I had the same thoughts too ... at first. But this little habit is no obsession. It's a reminder. That's right, a reminder – of God's faithfulness and provisions.

Every time my wife finds a penny, it's as if God placed it there just for her. It's a reminder that He is with her all the time – on the streets, in the park, wherever. Not only that, she finds pennies at significant times, too, like when we moved into a new home or when we prayed about an important matter or sought guidance for a major decision.

We now have a collection of both crusty-looking and shiny-looking pennies from all over the place. Really, it's more than a collection. It's an altar.

Building Altars

Throughout the Old Testament, when God did something significant in the lives of His people, they built altars to commemorate what He did. Noah built an altar to God as soon as he and his family stepped on dry land after the flood (Gen. 8:18-20). When God appeared to Abraham and told him that he and his offspring would inherit the Promised Land, he built an altar (Gen. 12:7). Later, his son, Isaac, did the same thing (Gen. 26:25).

These altars were more than symbolic. They were visual reminders of God's faithfulness and provision for His people. I can imagine that when people saw them – altars made with gigantic stones – they stopped and marveled at how good and faithful God is and has been throughout history.

That's what the pennies are: little copper altars to remind us that God is here and has not forgotten us or left us to fend for ourselves; that He cares deeply about every intricate detail of our lives. If we are to make it through the alleys of this life, we need reminders that tell us to keep going, others have gone this way before us, and, most importantly, that God has not abandoned us.

The Need for Prompters

How quickly we forget the promises of God and the truth that He will never leave us. And how often we feel the ache: alone, abandoned, confused, and lost in the fog. Lest you be too hard on yourself, the disciples themselves felt that way too shortly after they left the upper room. They listened as Jesus promised He would not leave them, but they did not really hear Him. When darkness fell, they all abandoned Him in the garden of Gethsemane, just as He said they would.

One moment Jesus was telling them, "Peace I leave with you; my peace I give to you" (John 14:27), and just moments later Peter pulled out a sword and sliced off a soldier's ear (John 18:10). How quickly he forgot!

How quickly we forget!

One moment we are drinking in deeply the love of Christ, holding on to Him and His Word, feeling victorious, untouchable by the world and completely satisfied; the next moment we are pulling out our hair from stress, feeling out of control, feeling absolutely dry like an old withered sponge. And yet both moments are all part of living in the alleys.

The ache never really goes away. It can be temporarily satisfied by God's presence. It can be massaged and stroked ever so gently, thus easing our discomfort, but it is always with us – at least in this life. And so we need prompters, little reminders that God is still here and still working.

Oftentimes when I have my prayer time in the morning, I pray that God would prompt me during the day to remind me that He is with me. I need a bit of a nudge because I know how easily I can lose my awareness of God's presence. We know and trust that He is with us at all times; but it's still important to recall His presence to our minds.

This is what Paul meant when he said we are to pray without ceasing (1 Thessalonians 5:17). We're not necessarily called to pray all day in some isolated place; rather, we are to be in a state of prayerfulness as we go through life, recalling to our minds God's presence and holding on to His promises.

Recognizing When God Speaks

I too have started the habit of finding pennies. To be honest it took me a while to find them. Angie found them effortlessly. I, on the other hand, needed a bit of help. I guess I really didn't see them. I chalked it up to it being her little habit and not mine. But I was wrong. God wanted me to find pennies as well. I just needed to open my eyes.

Slowly but surely I started to find pennies. And I always found one when I needed it the most, when I felt down or was struggling or just felt distant from God. Pennies became for me a reminder of God's love.

When I find a penny on the ground it's as if God is saying to me, "Hey, don't forget about Me. I am with you. I'm madly in love with you." Now I love finding pennies because it is God's promise to me. It's like seeing a rainbow in the sky after a big storm and being reminded of the promise God gave to Noah (and ultimately to us) that He wouldn't destroy the world by a flood ever again.

And a "penny" in this sense can be more than a coin; it can also be a person who often reminds us about God's love. I have such a "penny." His name is Pete and he lives in Michigan. He's been in ministry for a long time, is very wise, and hears from God. He is my sage. Every few weeks we talk on the phone and pray.

Pete's ministry is to help people really know God, to learn to hear from Him and to believe that He wants to speak to us. He has taught me how to tune my ear to God's voice and hear what He wants to say to me.

For me, trained in the many ways we use words, Pete has helped me realize the importance of listening – especially listening to God by quieting my mind and letting Him speak. It may sound kind of odd or perhaps overly-mystical to say that God wants to talk with us as friends talk to each other.

I was taught the importance reading God's Word, and that by reading His Word, I will hear His voice. And although this is true, Pete has broadened my perspective and has helped me to see how God can (and does) speak to us in a variety of ways. I believe He can speak to us through pennies, through the laughter of a child, through the smell of a bonfire, through the lapping of waves at our feet, a sunset, a friend, or through a good book.

The key is to learn to hear His voice and the specific ways He wants to speak to us. God wants to get our attention and remind us that He is here and at work all around us.

One night I was talking to Pete on the phone about faith and what God was showing me. That particular week I was going through a lot, wrestling with some things in my past and what it meant to be a man. Pete and I were talking and praying about this stuff – particularly my struggle with feeling I had to perform for God and feeling guilty for not measuring up. And in our time of silence, God said to me, "You are My son. You are not condemned. Let Me pursue you. Let Me love you." I couldn't believe it! Did God just speak to me those words? He did, and Pete confirmed it.

I'll never forget that night. God made it very clear how He felt about me. I don't have to try to perform to get His acceptance. I don't have to measure up to some lofty standard. I just have to let Him pursue me, let Him love me, and out of that, I am then freed up to love others.

Receiving Love

Pete once told me, "Dave, as much as you let God love you is as much as you will love others." I never thought of it like that before.

Really, how can we love another person unless we allow ourselves to be loved by God?

When Pete said that about God's love, it was as if a window in my soul opened up and let a wave of fresh, spring air in. *You mean*, I thought, *I don't have to earn God's love and try really hard to love others?* No. If I allow God to love me, His love will flow out of me and I will be free to love others in a selfless way.

For years I'd pray, "God, please help me to love other people more than myself. Help me to love my wife in the way You commanded me to." Although I meant it, I was still trying to perform for God. But now, thanks to God using Pete in my life, I pray that God would help me to first receive His love for me and then, and only then, will I be able to love others and my wife like I'm supposed to.

Little Reminders

I now find pennies all the time. It's not that they weren't there before, lying on the ground all dirty and scratched; I just didn't see them before. Sometimes you can see something but not really see it. This is how I feel about God. I feel like I see Him more than I did before as I struggle through this pilgrim life.

I'm convinced God wants us to see Him everyday and to listen to what He wants to tell us, and to allow Him to love us like crazy. He wants to speak clearly to us – through other people, through nature, through the city, through rainbows, through the smell of rain, through a warm cup of coffee, and on it goes.

The question is: Will we learn to listen to Him and see the "pennies" He has for us to find, the little reminders that He is always with us? This, I believe, keeps us going.

Oswald Chambers says, "It is ingrained in us that we have to do exceptional things for God – but we do not. We have to be exceptional in the ordinary things of life and holy on ordinary streets, among ordinary people – and this is not learned in five minutes."[1]

I hope and pray that today you will see a little clearer, even if it is just an ordinary day.

---

1 Chambers, *My Utmost For His Highest,* devotional on October 21.

Reflections From the Alley

1. How does God prompt you that He is there and is working?

2. How does God speak to you? Do you recognize His voice? If not, ask Him to speak to you. Ask Him to tell you how He feels about you. You will be amazed at what He says.

Lord, help me to recognize Your voice, to learn to hear You and see You in the everyday. Give me promptings that You are with me and are at work in my life. Adjust my eyes and open my ears. I ask this in Jesus' name, Amen.

Chapter 5

BLUES: What in the World Are We Doing Here?

"There's no way in the world I can feel the same blues the way I used to. When I play in Chicago, I'm playing up-to-date, not the blues I was born with. People should hear the pure blues - the blues we used to have when we had no money."

(Muddy Waters)

Every June Chicago holds the famous Blues Festival in Grant Park downtown. Thousands of fans and connoisseurs of the blues come out to cheer on their favorite blues players, men like Buddy Guy, B.B. King, and Johnny Winter.

It's safe to say the blues – although birthed in the Mississippi Delta – really took off in Chicago to become a worldwide phenomenon.

The phenomenon all started when Muddy Waters, the "father of the blues," migrated to Chicago from the South, and replaced his rural acoustic sound for a new, more robust urban sound by switching to the electric guitar in the late 1940's.

A movement was born, as many followed in Waters' footsteps and moved up to Chicago from their hot, rural homes in the Delta. This movement spread to many parts of the world, including Great Britain where it impacted bands like the Rolling Stones.[1]

Spiritual Blues

The blues movement also reached my world. I remember, as a fourteen-year-old kid, sitting in my room with a guitar in my hands, attempting to play along with my blues heroes. The year was 1989, and I had lots of zits and a short mullet, which I'm convinced would have received high ranking on www.ratemymullet.com.

---

1 Edmondstone, "History of Blues Music."

I would listen to their songs on my small tape deck for hours and play along. One such song was, "Still got the Blues," by Gary Moore. I would listen to that song over and over again, usually in the dark, whaling away on my shiny blue Kramer guitar.

I didn't think about the blues or what notes I was playing. I felt it. I'd shut the lights off, pull down the curtains, plug in my guitar and play my heart out. I believe I made it through the beginning years of adolescence (especially my ninth-grade year) by listening to and playing the blues. It was my escape and helped me endure the catastrophes of zits, bad hair, rejection by girls, and the bullies on my block.

Although human beings can and will assimilate to new environments, it doesn't eradicate our longing for place – that security and sense of belonging we all need. I think it's why blues music is so popular and has had such an effect on rock'n'roll.

We resonate with songs depicting a loss of love or a broken heart. We've all been there, right?

Sociologists tell us every person needs a place, somewhere they feel safe and loved and accepted. Without this, we feel un-human. Desperate. This is why following Jesus in our culture can be so hard ... we are out of place. We have the spiritual blues.

So how do we deal with our personal blues and a faith that seems so out of place in the world?

Tents

The Apostle Paul gives us a good picture of our predicament. "For while we are in this tent, we groan and are burdened, because we do not wish to be unclothed but clothed with our heavenly dwelling ..." (2 Corinthians 5:4).

Paul Minear says, "The church is by its very nature composed of tent dwellers."[2]

If you've spent any time camping – even if you're an outdoor fanatic – there's nothing quite like coming home, taking a hot shower, and sleeping in your own bed.

---

2 Frost and Hirsch, *The Faith of Leap*, 63.

I think this is what Paul's getting at. While we are here on earth it's like backpacking through the woods, setting up camp, tearing it down the next day, and moving on. The more we do this, the more we long for our bed, for light at the click of a switch, and for our fridge.

How We Make It

Let's go back to the story of the Last Supper and the events that unfolded in the upper room. Jesus was attempting to prepare His disciples for His departure. (They had been on the go – "camping" – with Jesus for three years.)

He knew their fears, their what-ifs, their ache. And He knows ours, too. To this He says, "Peace I leave with you; my peace I give you. I do not give to you as the world gives. Do not let your hearts be troubled and do not be afraid." (John 14:27).

So what does Jesus leave us while we groan in our tents? Peace. Not just any peace – His peace. The world promises to give a lot, but it does not come through. It promises instant gratification, pleasures, and security. But with all of those things, the ache still remains. The desire and the newness wear off. The new relationship, the new job, the great vacation you spent years saving for all wear off. What are we to do? What were the disciples in the upper room to do? Cling to the peace that Jesus gives. His peace. His presence. His peace is not of this world. It's heavenly. This is how we make it.

The Reason We Have the Blues

We find ourselves in interesting and desperate times, and with desperate times comes the temptation to buy into so-called promises for relief and security.

Republicans and Democrats are duking it out over which side is right and who's at fault for our over-spending and debt. A new political leader emerges, proclaiming lofty declarations of how he or she will be the one to get America back on track.

I honestly think most people around the world are tired of the false promises made by their governments and political leaders. Antigovernment protests and oftentimes acts of violence are occurring all over the Middle East, in Europe, and in North America.

In contrast to what we've been told, conditions in the world are not improving, nor are they supposed to. God's people know this; they have always been in displacement.

Days before the Passover meal, Jesus spoke to His disciples about all that must happen before He came back to earth and claim His throne as its rightful King. False prophets would rise up, lawlessness would increase, love will grow cold, wars and rumors of wars will abound, famines and earthquakes will happen – need I go on? (See Matthew 24).

Of course Jesus does not say when this will happen, but it will happen, and that His followers must "endure to the end" and "be on the alert" (Matthew 24:13; 24:42).[3]

And one of the ways we endure and stay on the alert is to hold on to His peace, the "peace of God, which transcends all understanding" which "will guard your hearts and your minds in Christ Jesus" (Philippians 4:7).

Holding On

We must be on guard against all of the false promises of peace we hear on the news, in movies, and, unfortunately, from the pulpits of preachers proclaiming wealth and prosperity. Jesus told His disciples He would not leave them as orphans and that He would come back. He told them to "remain in [His] love" (John 15:9).

He promised the coming of the Holy Spirit, and He urged them to love one another. But He also said, "I have told you these things so that you may have peace. In this world you will have trouble. But take heart! I have overcome the world" (John 16:33).

I've talked with countless people – many of them immigrants and refugees – who have endured horrific circumstances. I think of a Burmese Christian I know, who, along with her family, walked through the thick jungles of Burma for three weeks. They avoided soldiers by

---

3 NASB.

hiding in bushes. They made it by holding on to the peace of Christ, believing that He would protect them and lead them to safety.

Blues music is something you feel when you listen to it. It has this certain pull, drawing you into something much larger than yourself. You can get lost in the music. In a similar way, we need to get lost in God's peace, promised by Christ the night before His gruesome death and days before His triumphant resurrection.

Is life messy, difficult, unpredictable, and even downright nasty? You bet. But Jesus promises His peace – a peace that can get you through anything and surpass any circumstance, trial or disappointment.

With the peace of Christ we can make it in this darkening world, and deal with our longing for the world that is to come, the world for which we were made.

Reflections from the Alley

1. How have you experienced the peace of Christ in your life?

2. How does having spiritual blues help you live an effective life on earth?

Lord, You have set eternity on my heart. You have made me for Yourself and to live with You in Your perfect world. But I am here now, frail and weak and burdened, and I have bought into the lies of the world and its false promises. Forgive me and help me to hold onto Your peace, especially when things are difficult. Thank You, Jesus, that You are peace. In Your name, Amen.

Chapter 6

WISDOM: Learning to Live Outside the Net

> "May it be when darkness falls,
> Your heart will be true...
> You walk a lonely road,
> Oh how far you are from home"
> (Enya, *The Lord of the Rings*)

Author Philip Yancey says there are two days that have "earned names" on the church calendar: Good Friday and Easter Sunday. "Yet in a real sense," he writes, "we live on Saturday, the day with no name. What the disciples experienced in small scale – three days, in grief over one man who had died on a cross – we now live through on a cosmic scale. Human history grinds on, between the time of promise and fulfillment ... It's a good thing to remember that in the cosmic drama, we live out our days on Saturday, the in-between day with no name."[1]

One day this no-name Saturday will end and Easter Sunday – on a cosmic scale – will burst forth and become a reality. In the meantime, stuck in our Saturday existence, we wait for Easter Sunday to dawn with a mixture of hope and oftentimes disorientation.

This is what happens to many refugees when they are resettled to their new environment. Once the newness wears off – and, in this economy, it wears off pretty fast – the individual or family feel out of control. They don't know how to move forward and feel a sense of purposelessness, lost in a haze of uncertainties.

I'll never forget the words of one of my clients, an Iraqi Christian, who couldn't find a job and provide for his children. The result for him was disorientation and shame. He said, "I'd rather die quickly in my country than slowly in America."

Although you may not have had to flee your country and live as a refugee, I'm sure you too at times have felt disoriented.

---

1 Yancey, *The Jesus I Never Knew*, 275.

So if we live out our days in an unnatural environment, between the cross and the empty tomb, how are we to make it? I suggest the answer is found in one word: wisdom.

Practical Living

Wisdom can be defined as knowledge that is practical, full of insight and "good sense."[2] Jesus taught His disciples how to live outside of the nest, outside of the comfort zone of His guidance and leadership, and, ultimately, how to follow Him after He was gone. He taught them how to live practically, how to handle life with wisdom.

Discipleship – the act of following Jesus – is learning to follow Him in an unnatural environment, one in which, Jesus tells us, people will hate and persecute us (John 15:18-19). "I chose you out of the world, because of this the world hates you" (15:19b).[3]

Journey

The late biblical scholar, Robert E. Webber, says the word discipleship literally means "to follow after," and "implies the Hebraic concept of journey and walk."[4] Similarly, Bible scholar Ralph Gower, says that in Bible times, "The streets were so narrow that if two people went together, they had to go in a single file line. To follow after a person was to go with them."[5]

Unfortunately, many of us have been taught that discipleship is something we learn, a class we attend, or a sermon series at church. It often falls into the category of the linear. Discipleship, however, is much more than what we know. It is a journey, a pursuit. It's going with Jesus.

---

2 Merriam-Webster, "Wisdom."

3 NASB.

4 Webber, *Ancient Future Evangelism*, 22.

5 Gower, *The Essential Bible*, 155.

When I talk to my Muslim friends about the Christian faith, I don't talk about a religion or system. I talk about a Person, Jesus, and that following Him is a journey.

People from the Middle East get the idea of journey and pilgrimage. They typically don't think in terms of systems and formulas as Westerners do. For them, life is more narrative, more story-drenched, and definitely more community-oriented.

This is why many immigrants who come to America seek out the places or neighborhoods where people from their country live and move there. It's why many Somali refugees in America stay one or two years in a city, and then migrate to another city looking for better work and cheaper cost of living.

I believe Jesus spent three years with His disciples in an experiential way, even in a somewhat nomadic way. They never stayed in one place too long. They traveled by sea, to the mountains, to the desert, and even to "the other side of the tracks" where the Samaritans, the arch enemy to the Jews, lived.

Jesus did not teach His guys rules and policies. He told stories. He took them to new places and thrust them into risky environments. He even sent them out in pairs to do what He was doing (see Luke 10).

To know about Jesus, then, is not enough. We need to experience Him, to walk after Him. To know someone (including some things about them) doesn't necessarily mean you have a relationship. I've met a lot of people through events, speaking at different churches, and hosting mission groups. But that doesn't mean I have a close relationship with them.

We are all tempted to turn to formulas or a quick-fix. This is why self-help books and seven-steps-to-improve-your-life sermons are so popular. We like the easy way out, the way of minimal discomfort and pain.

But the truth is, the easy way out and a quick-fix are not the answer, especially if we're going to follow Jesus in displacement. This is why we need to experience Christ – to have a real relationship with Him.

Divine Wisdom

James understood this when he wrote his letter to the early Christians who faced all kinds of opposition. In essence, James reminded believers what Jesus taught: that they will face trials and challenges in a world that is utterly against them. And so James challenges us to tap into deep and real wisdom, the kind of wisdom, as he says, "comes from heaven," and is "first of all pure; than peace-loving, considerate, submissive, full of mercy and good fruit, impartial and sincere" (James 3:17).

The book of James is the New Testament equivalent to the Old Testament book of Proverbs. If you read it in one sitting, I think you will see the theme of divine wisdom clearly expressed. James challenges us to see that the truth of the gospel is not sustainable or real if we don't know how to live it out.

James warns us that faith by itself is dead. It must be accompanied by action. And this is where wisdom comes in. The question I believe James challenges us with is: How do we live out divine wisdom in a sin-filled world?

A Lesson from Birds

It may seem cruel, but sometimes the mother bird has to push her babies out of the nest if they're ever going to learn to fly. When a bird is a newborn, it is called a nestling. The nestling is pink with little or no feathers and must remain in the nest. The baby bird's parents know this and do everything they can to ensure the little one's safety.

A fledgling, on the other hand, is a baby bird that is older and more developed. Fledglings have feathers and can hop around the nest. When Mom and Dad see this, it's time their babies left. They give the baby a little shove and she is forced to fly. A fledgling on its own is way too comfortable in that cozy nest and will never learn to fly unless it's pushed.[6]

---

6 From an online article posted by the Animal Welfare League of Arlington, VA. http://www.awla.org/baby-birds.shtml.

The same principle is true for us, as it was for the disciples in the upper room. They were in the nest for three years and the day had come for the big push. And oh, what a push it was! In fact, it pushed them all to flee in disbelief and fear when the soldiers came after Jesus.

Under Pressure

James says true wisdom is proven when darkness falls: "Consider it pure joy, my brothers, whenever you face trials of many kinds, because you know that the testing of your faith develops perseverance" (James 1:2). *The Message* paraphrase of that verse says, "You know that under pressure, your faith-life is forced into the open and shows its true color. So don't try to get out of anything prematurely. Let it do its work so you become mature and well-developed, not deficient in any way" (4:3-4).

God doesn't want us to take shortcuts. He wants us to grow. I may be an amazing guy when I am by myself praying, reading, writing, filled with all of God's goodness and love. But the moment real life faces me – something happens in my family, I get a nasty email, I am criticized – that's when the real me steps forward. This, I think, is James' point.

> But God wants us out of the nest, where real life is, where we have to trust Him as if our life dependent on it."

When life hits us – real life, not the fluffy, pretend kind – how do we respond? We don't like to be pushed out of the nest. We like the nest. It's warm and cozy and smells nice, not to mention we're well fed. But God wants us out of the nest, where real life occurs, where we have to trust Him as if our life depended on it – which it does.

To do this requires wisdom from above. It requires a deep trust in God's presence as we live out our days in a hostile environment. Jesus promised the disciples the Holy Spirit who would guide them. He knew it would be hard and that they would be tested.

But the truth is, we would never trust God if we lived in the nest. Why would we have to? The disciples were forced to deal with their fears, their disbelief, and their sorrow, because Jesus pushed them out of the nest.

Saturday must have been the longest day to them – the day after their beloved Rabbi was nailed to a tree and crucified. But Saturday didn't last forever. And Saturdays won't last forever for us, either.

Our Hope

Paul says our hope of eternal life is found in the resurrection, and nowhere else: "If only for this life we have hope in Christ, we are to be pitied more than all men" (1 Corinthians 15:19). If there were no Easter Sunday, there would be no hope. How quickly the disciples' grief turned to joy when they embraced their beloved Rabi in His resurrected state! Now they had all the proof they needed that He was indeed their God and their King.

What Christ's resurrection meant for His disciples, so the promise of His return means for us. When He rose from the dead, their Saturday of disorientation ended – while ours will continue until He does return. Wisdom, then, is learning to be patient as we at the same time yearn for God to hasten that day, when the sufferings of our fallen world will finally cease.

Wisdom challenges us to hold on to God with everything we've got, in good times and bad. It means living each day intentionally, remembering what Jesus did for us and holding on to what He's promised us. John Salhamer writes, "Where, then, does the hope of the Christian lie? Like all biblical wisdom (cf. Ecclesiastes 12:13-14), for James the hope lies in the future fulfillment of God's eternal plan."[7]

---

7 Sailhamer, *NIV Compact Bible Commentary,* 576.

Reflections from the Alley

1. How does God push you out of the nest? What is He trying to show you?

2. Write down a few areas of your life that you need God's wisdom. Pray about each of these and ask Him to guide you.

Lord, help me to follow You each and every day. I know that true faith and wisdom is learning how to follow You no matter how hard life gets. Lord, the truth is, I need Your push. I get so comfortable sometimes and stop depending on You. Give me the wisdom to see where I need to grow and change. Help me to know Your presence more and more each day. In Your name, Amen.

To this point, we've tried to understand why God allows us to be displaced persons – living in an unnatural and disoriented state. Next we will look at God's purpose in our displacement: the call to bless.

BLESSING

SECTION TWO

SECTION 2

BLESSING

Blessing: *noun*
1. The act or words of a person who blesses.
2. Approval or good wishes.

I am convinced that one of the main reasons God allows us to struggle and work out our faith in this life is so that we can be a blessing to others. To bless others is to give them something at no cost to them and with no strings attached. It's giving in its purest form: solely for benefit of the other person.

Called to Bless

You see this principle throughout the Bible. God's people are called to bless. In the Old Testament book of Jeremiah, for example, God's people were sent into exile, displaced persons in a foreign city called Babylon.

Rather than complain about their plight, or dissociate from their new environment, God wanted them to assimilate. And so God wrote them a letter – through His prophet, Jeremiah – about how He wanted them to adjust to their new surroundings:

"'Build houses and settle down ... Increase in number there; do not decrease. Also, seek the peace and prosperity of the city to which I have carried you into exile. Pray to the Lord for it, because if it prospers, you too will prosper'" (Jeremiah 29:5, 7). In a word, God wanted His people to bless their new city and its people – a people, by the way, who had destroyed their beloved city, Jerusalem, and had taken them captive. (I will discuss this in more detail later in the book.)

God allows us to become displaced and disoriented, not because He wants to us to live aimless and embittered lives, but rather so that He can conform us even more to His will, His purposes.

Why?

So that we can then impact the world around us. God wants us to be people who give and who love with no strings attached. And oftentimes that doesn't happen until God shakes things up a bit and gets us to take our eyes off of ourselves.

My friend and former co-worker, Fiko, is a person I deeply admire. He's someone who's endured so much in his life and through it all has learned to use his life to bless others.

Beautiful Times

We all desire life to be pleasant, to enjoy friends and family and a good meal. For Fiko, this was a reality. Although his childhood was difficult, he pushed through and created a good life for himself.

"I was born in the most western part of Bosnia, near the border of Croatia," he said. "My parents divorced when I was nine months old. I was raised by my grandparents in a small village near my hometown. I was happy there because I had lots of friends and a good support system from my family."

After Fiko graduated from high school, it was mandatory for him to join the then-Yugoslavian Army. Fiko fulfilled his duty, got out of the army, got a good job, and got married. "It was beautiful times," he said. "We were happy. We had a house and two children."

Forced to Flee

But then a shadow covered the land and brought darkness to Fiko's family – and to so many others – who were happy and secure. In the wake of the breakup of Yugoslavia, and the Serbs' rejection of the referendum of independence implemented by the Socialist Party of Bosnia and Herzegovina, war broke out in April of 1992.

Sarajevo was bombed and besieged. Massive destruction, ethnic cleansing, and mass rape were rampant. It was a dark time. The "stupid" war, Fiko said, "ruined our way of life forever. And through the struggle of war I was forever disabled and together with my family and 25,000 of our townspeople were forced to flee to the neighboring country of Croatia."

Unfortunately, due to bad medical conditions as a result of the war, Fiko's leg had to be amputated. "For a long period of time we lived in a refugee camp in Croatia," he said. "It was uncertain that we would be going back home."

But throughout this experience, Fiko and his family remained strong. They were stripped of everything they had known. But they were alive. And they had hope.

"We were strong and full of life; we lived in fields, near roads and in tents. The Red Cross and the UNHCR came to our aid and supported us with food and shelter through the whole ordeal. They also gave us the opportunity to come to the United States as refugees and we accepted."

Giving Back

In the mid-1990s and into the Millennium, thousands of Bosnian refugees poured into cities such as Chicago, St. Louis, Hamtramck (in Detroit), and Fort Wayne, Indiana. The *New York Times* states that by as early as 1995, "the State Department resettled 131,000 refugees from war-torn Bosnia and Herzegovina in the United States. More than 9,000 were placed in Chicago, many of them clustered in the poorer quarters of the city's North Side."[1]

And it was in Chicago where Fiko and his family began the daunting task of rebuilding their lives. They lived in a small one-bedroom apartment in Albany Park, an ethnically diverse neighborhood on Chicago's northwest side.

"I thank the United States government for giving us the opportunity for a better way of life away from our pains of war," said Fiko. "When we arrived it was hard times for my family, getting used to the way of life, learning a new language, and figuring out how to support my family since I was physically disabled."

Although life in America was anything but a "dream" for Fiko, he decided he wanted to do something to help others who had suffered as he had. "After two years in Chicago, I was able to get a job, to work for

---

1 Clemetson, "Bosnians in America: A Two-Sided Saga."

the same organization, World Relief Chicago, that helped bring my family and me to the United States."

Fiko was hired as a caseworker to help other refugees in the same way that he had been helped. "As a caseworker," he said, "I feel my life experience has helped me a lot in my line of work, where now I can provide good advice, help people understand and utilize all of the things that the Refugee Program offers so they can get back on their feet faster."

Fiko is an amazing man and a good friend. I deeply admire him. Rather than become embittered in what he faced as a displaced person, he chose to assimilate into a new environment and take what he's gone through and use it for good.

Instruments of Blessing

I am convinced that one of God's main purposes in the world is to use His people as instruments of blessing. Thousands of years ago, God chose one man, Abraham, and said: "Leave your country, your people and your father's household and go to the land I will show you. I will make you into a great nation and I will bless you, I will make your name great, and you will be a blessing" (Genesis 12:1-2).

Think about what was asked of Abraham:

- Leave everything familiar to you and live as a displaced person (which he did, living out of tents).
- Go to an unknown place (which the Lord would reveal to him in time).
- Be a blessing to others. Through Abraham's trust in God, he would not only be blessed but bless others as well.

"The story of the Bible," writes Erwin McManus, "is God's intention to bring the nations to himself."[2] God chose a man (Abraham) and from him formed a nation (Israel) in order to reveal Himself to the world. More than that, Abraham was a picture of what faith looks like.

---

2 McManus, *An Unstoppable Force,* 117.

It is a picture of God's blessing which was ultimately fulfilled and embodied in the Person of Jesus – the greatest blessing in all of history.

God allows us to be displaced and outside of our comfort zone – just like Abraham – not only so our faith can grow, but so we can have maximum influence on people around us. God wants to use our lives – all of our struggles, upbringing, personalities, gifts, and dreams – and use them to bless others.

We are called – like Fiko and Abraham – to allow God to take our displacement and put it to good use for the benefit of others. The question we have to ask ourselves is: Are we willing to trust God and step out into the unknown? Are we willing to let God use us as instruments of blessing? I hope to help you find the answer to those questions in the chapters that follow.

Chapter 7

HOSPITALITY: The Calling to Bless

"Christ is in the person of every guest, and every stranger is Christ."
(Celtic Saying)

I'd like to paint for you a picture of the world and how God wants to use you to impact it.

Imagine you were invited to a feast. The feast was held in a large banquet room with a roaring fire beautifully enclosed in a stone fireplace, and your favorite types of food was served. The room was warm and cozy and the food was brought out on the finest china you could imagine – and it was all for you. As you ate and had your fill, you noticed some movement outside of the banquet room. There were people outside peering in the window.

You could tell they were hungry, their longings evident as they fixated on every bite you took. Here you are, given the feast of your life and are now full, and you see hungry people looking in, noticing there's plenty of food uneaten.

What would you do? Invite these hungry people in? Take some food to them? Or would you just sit there, content and full, hoping those people would just go away?

Something to Give

I suggest this is a picture of our culture. We live in an age where people are starving. Although we have seemingly endless pleasures, attractions, comforts and resources, people are withering all around us. And it's not just lost people who don't know Christ. Many believers in today's world feel hopeless. Their faith has been severely tested and they're not sure how much more they can take.

The only way they can make it, then, is to desperately hold on to Christ and His promises, and to believe He is still at work in the world and wants to use His people to make a lasting and eternal difference in people's lives. But in order to do that, we who are His followers, have to believe that we are full – satisfied in Him – and have something to give.

The line of thinking goes like this:

1. If we are in Christ, then we are full. "We have been made complete in Christ" (Colossians 2:10).[1]
2. Because we are full, we can now share with others who are in need (empty and hungry).
3. In meeting people's needs, we fulfill the Law of Christ – "Love your neighbor as yourself" (Galatians 5:14).

Many Christians in our day and age, however, have not (a) tasted that God is good and are therefore not satisfied or full; and (b) are unaware that starving people are all around them; and that (c) they can be used as God's instruments to minister to them.

This brings me to the purpose of this section: We are called to bless others. So far we've seen how disorientation is the environment God places us in to teach us to trust Him, so that He can mold us into the men and women He desires us to be. And one of the main ways we bless others is by showing them *hospitality*.

Offering Warmth

So what is hospitality and how do we live it out?

There was a day (if you can imagine!) before electricity, iPhones, plasma TV's, the internet, and all of our other modern conveniences, when the hearth was prominent. Today, that's a word we don't hear very often outside of watching a very old movie or reading a Charles Dickens novel.

But for thousands of years a hearth was the center of the home. Its Latin root, in fact, means something that is central or focused. Basically, the hearth was a stone-lined fireplace and oven, used to both heat the home and feed those in the home, and was usually centrally placed.

---

1 NASB.

When I think of a hearth, I think of warmth; I think of a family gathered around a fireplace, telling stories, listening to the fire pop and crackle. I also think of hospitality, a concept that is sadly out of vogue in our modern Christianity. And yet I believe hospitality is vital if we are to be effective followers of Jesus.

My friend, Lewie, in Chicago has taught me that hospitality and discipleship go hand in hand. He once told me, "Once I started understanding the importance of hospitality, and I started cooking meals and serving, it changed the whole dynamic of my group."

"Hospitality bestows value, honor and a sense of belonging to a person," he says. "Hospitality is about being a servant and laying down your life for others." In its truest sense, the practice of hospitality is opening your life to others, serving others, loving others – creating a hearth. It is learning to share out of our fullness in Christ to those in need.

Adoption

Hospitality is in the heart of God. We are *adopted* into God's family. Jesus said to His disciples in the upper room, "If anyone loves Me, he will obey my teaching. My Father will love him, and we will come to him and make our home with him" (John 14:23).

This is amazing to think about: God wants to make His home in us, to dwell there, to be at the center, to be the *hearth* of our lives.

Lewie pointed out to me that hospitality is a major theme in Luke's gospel. Luke starts with Jesus' birth in a cave with animals (a lack of hospitality), and he ends with Jesus being the host and His followers recognizing Him in "the breaking of the bread" (Luke 24:35).

It was because of these conversations with Lewie, and watching my wife serving others through cooking and baking, inviting refugees, immigrants, and the poor into our home, that I started reading and studying about hospitality. My findings led me to see that hospitality is so much more than a word we see in hotel brochures or at a church's welcome center. It is (or should be) a way of life and a vital part of the life of faith for *every* believer.

People in our culture are desperately looking for hearth, a place of warmth, safety, and refuge. This must be a major focus for us as followers of Jesus. The lonely, the broken, the sojourner, the stranger are all looking to belong, looking for a place where they can feel welcomed, safe, and cared for.

Interestingly, the biblical word for hospitality in Greek is: *philoxenia* – "love of strangers." It combines two words: *philo,* meaning affection or brotherly love, and *xenon,* meaning alien or stranger. The Latin root of hospitality is *hostis,* which means "stranger" or "enemy." From that we get *hospitem,* Latin for guest or host. And from these roots, we get such English words as *hospital, host, hostel,* and *hotel.* Hospitals, in fact, were originally hospices (places of refuge and safety) for pilgrims traveling to the Holy Land.

What are some practical ways we can offer warmth to those around us? How can we be a personal refuge to those in need?

Practical Ways to Bless

Speaking. One of the best ways to bless another is through our words. Scripture calls us to build up or edify others (See Romans 14:19). Interestingly, the English word "edify" comes from the *aedes,* Greek for "hearth." Our words, then, should be warm and used to build up others. As Paul says: "Watch the way you talk. Let nothing foul or dirty come out of your mouth. Say only what helps, each word a gift." (Ephesians 4:29).[2] Words have the power to build people up or tear them down. Let's use our words to bring life to others.

Listening. Not only should our mouths be used to bless, so should our ears. I have found when we listen to someone – I mean, *really* listen, with the intent of understanding and not waiting until they're done so we can speak – it truly blesses the person. I've learned this working with refugees and immigrants. Often what they really need is a listening ear. I remember when my friend from Liberia described (in vivid detail) what life was like growing up in the 1990s under the monstrous regime of Charles Taylor's rebel movement. "Dead bodies were everywhere," he said, "just like in the movie *Hotel Rwanda.*" My friend was fortunate enough to escape to Ghana. I had no idea what to say in reply. I just listened. And that meant the world to him.

---

2 The Message.

Inviting. Hospitality means moving toward someone with the purpose of accepting, valuing, and engaging. It's all about relationship. People want to feel they matter to you. And one of the best ways to show that is by inviting them into your lives. Let them see you – the real you – who struggles and doubts and, at times, wonders if this whole faith journey is legit. The last thing people want, especially if they are seeking out who Jesus is, is someone who appears to have all the answers and seems to be unscathed by the world and all the pain in life. Invite them into you: your struggles, fears, hopes, dreams. Let them see the you God's made you to be.

Eating. One of the best ways to bless someone and get to know them is to share a meal with them. If you read through the gospels, you'll see Jesus spent a lot of time eating with people. He even invited Himself over to eat with them. (See the story of Zacchaeus in Luke 19). In many cultures throughout the world, when you share a meal with someone it means you are "in." You become a part of their family. One of the greatest ways I've seen God work in my life is when I share a meal with someone. Just the other day, in fact, as we drank coffee, my friend from Yemen told me I am like a brother to him and he loves me. It was a powerful moment. I really don't think I've done anything to cause him to feel the way he does. But the Lord reminded me of the many times I've listened to my friend pour his heart out and the many times we've shared a meal together.

Blessing others is a powerful force. It changes people's lives. When people sense they are loved and valued for who they are and not for what you can get from them, it speaks volumes. People want to feel our message, our lives, our presence. They don't want a sales pitch. They want to be cared for. That's what blessing is all about. It's real. And it changes people.

The question for this second section is: How are we to bless one another? What does it look like? Can we learn from the stories of others in how they live out blessing? I think so.

Reflections From the Alley

1. Think of a way you can bless somebody today or this week. Use one of the above examples or come up with your own. Write it down here.

Lord, You have given me so much. You have given me life both here and eternally. I could never repay You for that. But I do want to make my life count. I'd ask that You'd use me to be a blessing to others. Help me to invite people into my life, and ultimately, into Your life. Use me, Lord, for Your purposes and work. In Jesus' name. Amen.

Chapter 8

PLACEMENT: God at Work in the Margins

"Strangers are 'people without a place.' To be without a place means to be detached from basic, life-supporting institutions – family, work, polity, religious community, and to be without networks of relations that sustain and support human beings." (Christine D. Pohl)

Have you ever wondered why God places you in various situations? Or why He placed you in your particular family or culture or city? As I think back on my life and the situations that God placed me in – even the times when I questioned or struggled – I see how God has both led me and blessed me, and in turn through me, blessed others.

I remember the time I was offered a job in Ohio a few months after I graduated from college. The job sounded great; it aligned with my passions, and I would be close to friends. But something inside told me to hold off and wait. So I told my potential new boss, "I think I want this job but if you could just give me one more day to decide, that would be great." He agreed.

I'm so glad I waited ... because that next morning I was offered a different job as a youth pastor in Michigan. When the interview was over, I knew God wanted me at the church in Michigan and not in Ohio, although at the time I had no idea why. Now I know why. It was where I would meet my wife.

Reception and Replacement

Placement is the opposite of displacement. *Placement* means the act of putting something in a certain or particular place. In the world of refugee resettlement, we use the term Reception and Placement (R&P).[1]

---

1 To learn about Reception and Placement, check out information from the U.S. Department of State: http://www.state.gov/j/prm/releases/onepagers/181046.htm.

R&P is a Department of State program that exists to help refugees in their admission to the United States. The program is implemented by a sponsoring agency, which is then responsible to ensure safe and secure services to the refugee within the first thirty to ninety days of their life in America.

When I worked with World Relief – one of the sponsoring agencies that receive R&P funding – I was responsible for cooperating with the guidelines of this program, which included placing refugees in affordable and safe housing, providing essential furnishings, food, adequate clothing, and so on.

The idea of placement is to ensure the refugee gets set up in a new home, receives food stamps, cash assistance, and medical help from the local social services office, applies for his or her social security card, and can begin the exciting yet daunting process of employment. The goal of resettlement is to help the refugee become self-sufficient. To do so, they must learn to assimilate into his or her new environment.

The Paradox of Assimilation

The great paradox of assimilation is: What are they assimilating into? Assimilation is a good thing, to be sure. It means we learn to absorb what's around us, to adapt, to be in harmony with the people and circumstances around us. The tricky thing with assimilation is to make sure what is absorbed is good and beneficial.

When God called Abraham out to an "unknown place" (Genesis 12:1), Abraham had to learn to adapt to the other cultures around him, while staying clearly focused on the task God gave him. The ultimate test came when God told him that he and his wife would have a son in their old age who would be the seed of God's new nation, Israel.

Fear

Even as we try to assimilate God's purposes for our lives, we can get off-track in our faith journey, and fail to see what His purposes are. Our displacement becomes too difficult, and we find ourselves taken in by the world and led away from God.

That's what happened to Abraham in Egypt. Shortly after God had called him to step out in faith, Abraham found himself in a new land with a new language and new customs. And he panicked. Things looked grim. There was a famine in the land. Abraham and his companions were weary from traveling, so they reached a compromise.

"As he was about to enter Egypt, he said to his wife Sarai, 'I know what a beautiful woman you are. When the Egyptians see you, they will say, 'This is his wife.' Then they will kill me but will let you live. Say you are my sister...'" (Genesis 12:10-13). What happened? Did God mislead Abraham? Was he somehow forced to manage things on his own and thus turn to self-protection?

No. He just didn't trust God. He let fear dictate. Abraham's faith was tested ... and in his first test, it seems, he didn't do so hot. And when the tests come our way, we often don't do so hot, either.

God wants us to assimilate into His purposes. The world says we can't trust God so we might as well try to get on with life, even if that means compromising here and there. So we take control. And when we do that, we miss out on God's blessing and being a blessing to others.

God's purpose was to use Abraham to be a blessing to many. And this is God's purpose for us as well. To be a blessing, however, means we must enter into God's purposes.

Invited In

God offers us the ultimate assimilation: He invites us into Himself. In this holy place, there is no fear, no what-ifs, no condemnation. Jesus spoke this invitation in the upper room on the night He was betrayed. Let His words sink into your heart. "We will come to *you* and make Our home [abode, special dwelling place] with *you*" (John 14:23).[2]

Placement means we have a place. We're invited in. We're invited into all of God: The Father, the Son, the Holy Spirit. We're invited into His family, both past, present, and future. Talk about having a place to live!

But the tricky thing – and the thing I think every believer in every age has wrestled with – is, how do we find our placement with God

2 Amplified Version, emphasis mine.

while we live displaced in this world? It's the great paradox of our faith. Jesus prays about this specifically, shortly after He and the disciples left the upper room and headed toward the garden outside the city. Consider His prayer in John 17:

- *Presence:* "They (the disciples) were yours; you gave them to me and they have obeyed your word" (v. 6, emphasis mine).
- *Protection:* "Holy Father, protect them by the power of your name" (v. 11). "My prayer is not that you take them out of the world but that you protect them from the evil one" (v. 15).
- *Usefulness:* "As you sent me into the world, I have sent them into the world" (v.17). "I pray also for those who will believe in me through their message" (v. 20).
- *Holiness:* "Sanctify them by the truth; your word is trust" (v. 17). "I have given them the glory that you gave me" (v. 22).

The Blessing of Margins

Jesus prayed for believers such as you and me so we would find our place in Him, and then from that place, touch the world around us.

One of the places where God is most active is the place of margins. "Margin" and "marginal" refer to borders or edges. God works at the edges of life, in the alleys, far away from the clout and the image and the prestige so esteemed by the world. God's people have always been marginalized. The Bible makes this clear and normative: We are called to the edges, like Abraham – to trust in a God of the edges who moves us and leads us in ways we can't comprehend, and in ways the world dismisses as crazy.

So if God is at work in the margins, then we should be, too. And let's face it: there are a lot of marginalized people out there. Jesus was always drawn to the outcast, to the one who was on the margins. The prostitutes. The tax collectors. The widow and the orphan.

When we seek to bless the marginalized among us, knowing that we too are strangers in a strange land, God shows up and transforms ... both them and us.

I am learning to trust in a God who wants to use our displacement and assimilate us into His place – a place of love, belonging, and compassion – so we in turn can help others assimilate into God's family.

It's never easy living in the margins, feeling strangely out of place and anxious about the future. But it's the best place for us to grow. It is the place of God's purposes. Faith means stepping out to the edge. It means taking risks like Abraham and being willing to go to unknown places. "The dock is the safest place for a ship, but that's not what ships are made for."[3]

Reflections From The Alley

1. How has God given you a holy place?

2. In what ways do you feel God is asking you to step out in faith into the edges or the unknown?

Lord, thank You that You dwell within me. You call me into unknown places so my faith will grow. Help me, Lord, to trust You in the margins and to see how You are at work there. Help me to find my place in You. And lead me to others that I may be a blessing to them and help them see the place You have for them. In Jesus' name, Amen.

---

3 Paulo Coelho, as quoted by Frost and Hirsch, *The Shaping of Things to Come*, 223.

Chapter 9

SEPARATION: *It's Only Temporary*

"Never be afraid of an unknown future to a known God."
(Corrie Ten Boom)

I once listened to an interview on the internet with J.R.R. Tolkien. The interviewer asked Tolkien about the Shire, the enchanted, sleepy village where his famous hobbits live in *The Lord of the Rings* trilogy. Tolkien said the Shire resembles the English countryside of his boyhood, evoking simplicity and refuge from the harsh realities of the Industrial Revolution and all of the factories it had spawned all across England. The Shire, in other words, evokes longing and, most importantly, home.

In Peter Jackson's film rendition of Tolkien's book, *Return of the King*, there is a great scene that captures this sense of longing and of home. Sam turns to Frodo on the dreaded slope of Morodor, only steps away from where the ring of power was to be destroyed, and says, "Mr. Frodo, do you remember the Shire?"

"It will be spring soon," Sam continues. "The orchards will be in bloom and the birds will be nesting in the hazel thicket."

At this, the exhausted and burdened Frodo looks up at Sam. A glimmer of hope softens Frodo's eyes.

"Do you remember the taste of strawberries?" Sam asks.

"Oh Sam," Frodo says, "I can't recall the taste of food. Not the sound of water or the touch of grass."[1] As he speaks, his eyes lose their softness and despair enters.

Sam's eyes intensify as he sees his beloved friend suffer under the weight of his burden. He cries out, "So let us be rid of it! I cannot carry it for you, but I can carry you!" And with that, he hoists Frodo onto his shoulders and starts to climb.

---

1 Jackson, *The Lord of the Rings: Return of the King.*

Anxiety

What a powerful picture of the reality we find ourselves in. Life and all of its burdens crash down on us, sometimes unbearably.

When new refugees or immigrants come to a new country, they feel a sense of separation.

I think this is also what happened to the disciples in the upper room. They experienced anxiety separation.

Anxiety separation is a common condition that many young children face when one or both parents leave the room, the house, the child in daycare, and so on. When my son, Luke, turned one, I noticed he would be anxious every time I'd leave the room or especially, when I'd leave the house. He would cry, not wanting me to leave

Research shows that separation anxiety is very normal, and even healthy, in a child's development. The child is showing his or her dependency on the parent and the need for security. However, some children experience severe separation anxiety and, despite the parents' best efforts, the symptoms can remain a long time. This is not the case with Luke, thankfully, as he's learned that when daddy or mommy leave the room or the house, they will be back.

Our Lot in Life

This is why Jesus allowed the disciples to go through this separation anxiety in the upper room and in the hours following. He said, "My children, I will be with you only a little longer" (John 13:33). It's Interesting that Jesus addressed the disciples "My children," – literally, "little children." I think Jesus knew His words would evoke anxiety. Think about it: they had been with Him for three years, they had left everything to follow Him. And now He's talking about leaving and that they wouldn't be able to find Him? Who wouldn't be anxious?

There comes a time in a new immigrant's journey, usually after six months or so, where they begin to assimilate – develop a sense of security, begin employment, get off welfare – but then something happens, and they hit a wall. They lose their first job, get sick, find out a loved one back home has died. They feel separated. Detached. Stuck. Now what? Assimilation turns to desperation.

Isn't this true for you and me? Life moves along, we learn to adjust, assimilate into our environment, and then – boom! – our world gets rocked. Something sets us off course.

For followers of Jesus, this is our lot in life. We and the world never truly assimilate. Sure, we learn to adjust, but something always happens – something God allows – which reminds us we are truly separated. Set apart. Different. The Bible is clear: We are to be in the world, but not of the world.

That's why we must ask ourselves what we are assimilating to? Is it Christ and His purposes? Or is it something else, like jobs or relationships or dreams? I think there are two ways to look at why God allows us to feel separate from the world around us:

Placement. God places us in difficult environments – in places that we in no way can handle on our own – so we will learn to trust in Him and find our meaning and hope in Him. Jesus says, "Blessed our those who are poor in spirit [i.e., people who acknowledge their need for God in order to make life work] will inherit the Kingdom" (Matthew 5:3).

Position. God sends us to difficult places so we can bless others and make a difference in their lives. He positions us to bless when we are empty of ourselves and full of Him.

Every person feels separate. Even unbelievers. They just don't know why. Christians are able to relate to people, to see them with the right perspective, because we know what the right perspective is – Jesus.

Perspective

Throughout the Scriptures, we are told to not lose perspective on the promise that the Messiah will come back and restore all things. We are told God will one day wipe away every tear and take away sin and death once and for all, that we will once again walk with God and with others in perfect harmony. (See Isaiah 25:7-8.)

Peter, writing to believers who were facing intense persecution under the Roman Empire, says: "But according to His promise we are looking for new heavens and a new earth, in which righteousness dwells" (2 Peter 3:13).[2] In the verses that follow, he also says that we are to be diligent in our patience for this to happen, keeping blameless and growing in our faith (3:14-18).

Great words, but hard to follow. And the reason is because we so easily forget these promises and grow weary under the pressures of this world. Like Frodo we forget the Shire, the taste of food, the flowers in the spring.

But our sojourn here is only for a short while; it's certainly not a place we'll be in forever.

When my wife or I leave the house, we tell our son, "Dadda (or Momma) will be right back." This is the essence of what Jesus was saying: "Guys, listen, I have to go. I have to show you the full extent of My love. I will be betrayed, die on a cross, and then be raised to life again and go home to My Father. But don't worry; it's only temporary. I will come back for you."

God gave us a place in His family. And while we are on earth, we are called to help other pilgrims, other displaced persons, find their place in God's family, too. Until people turn to Christ and allow Him to come in and make His home within them, they are homeless.

Separation anxiety will only last a little longer. We must, just like my son, have a childlike faith that our Lord will come back. Right now, we're apart and sometimes afraid. But it's only a temporary separation.

Reflections From the Alley

1. How have you experienced separation anxiety in your faith? What was it like?

---

2 NASB.

2. Name one person in your life who is separated from God and His family. Pray about how you can reach out to that person.

Lord, thank You for placing me in Your family. You've given me a home. Even when everything else in life is hard, I can always turn to You and find open arms. Help me, Lord, to show others this place – the place where Your love and grace abound. In Jesus' name. Amen.

Chapter 10

LOVE: God's Plan for a Broken World

"To love another person is to see the face of God."
(Victor Hugo)

Shortly after I became a follower of Jesus, I attended a Christian college in the Midwest. It was honestly a great experience where I grew a lot in my faith. During my freshman year, however, I felt a bit like an outsider compared to the other students around me.

Most of the guys on my hall came from strong Christian families in the Midwest. They had conservative views on life, knew what they wanted to do after they graduated, believed they would marry their high school sweetheart, or would meet a girl at the college who would, of course, join their life's pursuit. They were the kind of guys who were the youth group all-stars, the ones closest to the youth pastor and who always won at games like, Chubby Bunnies, where you wrap people up in toilet paper until they look like a mummy.

Don't get me wrong. I'm not in any way against youth group all-stars. I just grew up completely different from them.

For starters, I'm from the politically-charged DC area, where I was exposed to very liberal ideas. I didn't grow up in a Christian family, my parents' divorced when I was young, and I didn't know any hymns or popular Christian music artists.

For instance, one of my close friends in college mentioned the name Ray Boltz, a popular Christian singer. "What team does he play for?" I asked, showing my ignorance. My friend cracked up. The next day I found pictures of Ray Boltz all over my dorm room. But I honestly had no idea who the guy was, and really believed he played in the NFL.

My point is I felt a bit intimidated by all my friends who had grown up in good Christian families with both parents at home. In fact, I felt a bit jealous. I remember questioning God as to why I couldn't have grown up like they did. Why couldn't I have been normal like them? Why did I have to go through so much?

God's Higher Purpose for Pain

A few years later, I began to understand. My first job out of college was in the Detroit area where I served as a youth pastor at a church. Interestingly, a lot of kids who came to the youth group were from broken homes. I would meet with them and listen to their stories of struggle and pain and mistrust of authority figures, especially God.

> "I began to see that God uses our pain, our disappointments, our feelings of rejection, for a higher purpose - His redemptive purpose."

And one day it hit me: I had to go through what I went through in order to love these kids. They trusted me because they knew I understood where they were coming from. I told them quite frankly I didn't have the whole God-thing figured out, and that it's okay to question and struggle and doubt.

I began to see that God uses our pain, our disappointments, our feelings of rejection, for a higher purpose – for His redemptive purpose.

Paul writes, "Praise be to the God and Father of our Lord Jesus Christ, the Father of compassion and the God of all comfort, who comforts us in all our troubles, so that we can comfort those in any trouble with the comfort we ourselves have received from God" (2 Corinthians 1:3-4). *The Message* version says, "He comes alongside us when we go through hard times, and before you know it, he brings us alongside of someone else who is going through hard times so that we can be there for that person just as God was there for us" (vs. 4).

Pain and suffering and struggles can be used by God to do amazing things in this world. The key is to allow God to transform our suffering and use it for His work in people's lives. We must choose to allow God to comfort us, to be present in our lives, and allow Him to use our pain for His glory. If we don't, we will grow bitter, disillusioned, and we will believe the deadly lie that God is not fair and has abandoned us.

Places of Warmth

To bless others, then, is to allow God to take our brokenness and use it to help heal others – to funnel His love out of us and into others. Our lives become places of warmth and love for those who feel alone and crushed by life's coldness.

A few months ago, my wife got a text from a good friend in Chicago who had lost his fourteen-year-old nephew. He was crushed. His text said, "I'm devastated. I feel that my God has forsaken me."

So many people we know are facing hard times: terminal illness, marriage problems, the loss of a loved one, financial problems, a layoff. And the words we hear so often are, "I'm all alone." They are looking for warmth. For a shoulder to cry on. For understanding.

Loneliness

All of us face loneliness and loss. I know I have. When our son was born, my wife had a lot of complications. She was very sick, far from family, and needed help. I not only took off time from my social work job at the refugee agency, I took a month off from all of my responsibilities in ministry as well.

At the time, I was leading a house church in our neighborhood. I told the group I was taking time off to help my wife and tend to our newborn. You'd think they would understand. But they didn't. After a week or so, my wife and I found out that people in the church felt, as they put it, "abandoned." As a result, they were upset and thought we didn't care about them. One person in the church confessed he was angry and bitter toward me.

I was shocked. I couldn't believe it. My wife was crushed, too. There were no phone calls, nothing like "if you need anything at all ..." Nothing. We were alone, sleep-deprived; we felt isolated and very vulnerable. It was one of our darkest times. As a result, I started questioning being in the ministry. *What's the point?* I thought. *When others are in need, or hurting, I'm there for them.*

Learning to Love

A few months after this experience with our church, God spoke to me in a huge way.

It was a dreary day, like so many days in Chicago, and my soul matched the weather. I needed to get out of the office and clear my head. Mostly, I needed Jesus. I went to my car and I prayed: "Lord, speak to me. I feel so empty right now. I need You."

It just so happened I had a book in my car called *Inside Out* by Larry Crabb. So I picked it up and started reading. One particular paragraph leapt off the page. It was exactly what I needed. It was the Lord's words to me. My soul soaked in some rays of hope that dreary day, and I walked back to work rejuvenated. This is what I read:

> God wants to change us into people who are truly noble, people who reflect an unswerving confidence in who He is that equips us to face all of life and still remain faithful. Spirituality built on pretense is not spirituality at all. God wants us to be courageous people who are deeply bothered by the horrors of living as part of a fallen race, people who see, yet emerge prepared to live. Scarred, still troubled, but deeply loving. When the fact is faced that life is profoundly disappointing, the only way to make it is to learn to love. And only those who are no longer consumed with finding satisfaction now are able to love. Only when we commit our yearnings for perfect joy to a Father we have learned to deeply trust are we free to live for others despite the reality of a perpetual ache.[1]

I realized the reason God let me go through the disappointment, rejection and hurt was so I would learn to love. For so long I had attempted to find satisfaction and meaning in my ministry and role as a pastor. When it was stripped away, all I had to lean on was Christ.

God gave me a verse I clung to everyday – and which I still cling to – during that dark time: "… and in Him you have been made

---

1 Crabb, *Inside Out*, 19.

complete, and He is the head over all rule and authority" (Colossians 2:10).[2]

That's it: Christ is our fullness. We are complete in Him. To be complete means to lack nothing, to be whole. No wonder David wrote, "The Lord is my shepherd I shall not be in want" (Psalm 23:1). He's saying, "With God, I'm all set. I don't lack a thing."

We're Not All Right

The truth is, we're not all right. The world we live in is not all right. That is why we need Jesus. Until we realize this and stop looking at all the stuff the world says is important – what kind of smart phone we own, how many friends we have on Facebook, the size of the church we attend, the type of ministry or organization we lead, the type of family we come from – we are destined for buckets of loneliness and emptiness.

I think Jesus, more than anything in the upper room, wanted to teach His guys how to love. To do so, however, meant He had to strip away every false security or idea His disciples were holding on to – including how He was going to bring about His Kingdom. He said, "A new command I give you: Love one another. As I have loved you, so you must love one another. By this all men will know that you are my disciples, if you love one another" (John 13:34-35).

God wants us to be known by love. Christians, unfortunately, are often associated with things they are against – homosexuality, abortion, liberal political views, Islam. But when the world sees us, they should see we're deeply loving of all people, and desperately holding on to God in a world that is falling apart.

We Can Only Give What We Have

I am beginning to understand that all we go through in life is God's way of teaching us how to love both Him and others. We humans are a stubborn bunch, striving to figure out how to make life work to our

---

2 NASB.

betterment, trying to find as much ease and happiness as we can. But God wants us to operate by His way of life: love.

The truth is, we can only give what we have. If we don't allow God to love us, either because we are too proud or simply cannot believe that He would forgive and accept us, then we have nothing to offer the hurting and desperate people around us. We are hindered in our ability to bless others.

C.S. Lewis said, "He who loves, sees."[3] And we can only see and love others as much as we are willing to see within ourselves, allowing God to take our broken and messy life and use it to make the world a little more beautiful.

Reflections from the Alley

1. How have you seen God use difficult things in your life to help other people?

2. Why do you think God uses pain and struggle to teach us to love?

Lord, teach me how to love – a real, deep, genuine kind of love that makes a difference in people's lives. Help me see how You want to use my struggles and pain to help other people. Help me to find all my fullness and value in You. You alone meet all my needs. You alone complete me. And it's through Your life and Your love, that I can love others. Thank You, Lord. In Jesus' name, Amen.

---

3 Lewis, *George MacDonald*, xxvi.

Chapter 11

GIVING: Learning to Live an Abnormal Life

"Men need to know that life really is found in God. They also need to know that life at its highest is found when we give ours away on behalf of someone else." (John Eldredge)

In 1939 when the world was on the brink of World War II, C.S. Lewis preached a sermon at St. Mary's Church in Oxford. The sermon was then published and given the title, "Learning in War-Time." Because of the war, and the impending military draft, many Oxford undergraduates questioned whether or not they should continue on with their studies. Lewis addressed this: "The war creates no absolutely new situation; it simply aggravates the permanent human situation so that we can no longer ignore it. Human life has always lived on the edge of a precipice. Human culture has always had to exist under the shadow of something infinitely more important than itself. If men had postponed the search for knowledge and beauty until they were secure, the search would never have begun. We are mistaken when we compare war with 'normal life.' Life has never been normal."[1]

In this section of the book, I have attempted to express the truth that once we face the fact that we are displaced people and life can be profoundly disappointing and hard, we can then move on toward loving and serving others, believing God can and will use our brokenness and pain to bless others.

But the subtle lie we believe, one I think Lewis addressed so clearly, is that of wanting a "normal life."

War Zone

Early on in my marriage, my wife and I struggled with how to connect and communicate and live together as husband and wife. I

---

1 Lewis, *The Weight of Glory*, 49.

remember thinking, *Why can't we just have a normal marriage? Why can't we be like ... so and so?*

It wasn't until a few years later when I started counseling with couples to prepare them for marriage, that I realized there is no such thing as a normal marriage. Every marriage is hard. Life is hard. There is nothing normal about it.

The truth is, we live in a war zone. Satan is the "prince of this world" (John 14:30). Although God is sovereign and in control of everything, Satan has authority on earth. And he uses that authority to do everything he can to turn us away from God, from each other, and from loving and being loved. The book of Revelation says Satan is "the accuser of our brothers, who accuses them before our God day and night..." (Revelation 12:10).

Unraveled

There is nothing normal about that. After Adam and Eve succumbed to Satan's deception back in the Garden of Eden (Genesis 3), everything began to unravel. What was once normal – God's perfect creation – is now diseased by sin.

Following their banishment from Eden, Cain killed Abel out of jealousy and hatred. This is where you and I live now – east of Eden, where the soil is soaked with the blood of hatred, war, poverty, sickness and death.

As I mentioned before, my wife and I have many friends who suffer from terminal diseases, broken relationships, the loss of a family member – it's disheartening. But it's reality. There is a dark cloud hovering over our world. Satan is not letting up. He knows his time is short and that one day the King will come back and destroy him forever.

In the meantime, here we are, attempting to live effective lives in a very messed up and abnormal world. To do so, I believe, requires us to dispel three very common (and very deadly!) lies the enemy throws at us.

1. God Cannot Be Trusted

More and more I am hearing this from believers. "I don't know how much more I can take. Does God really care?" I think one of the deadliest lies Satan throws at us is that God cannot be trusted. Isn't this what he did with Adam and Eve? "Did God really say ... ?" (Genesis 3:1).

"Did God really say he loves you?" "Did God really say He'd forgive you for that?" "Do you think you can really trust Him?"

These are the enemy's classic lines, and he uses them to reel us in. Yet, we believe life should be normal. We think it should work out a certain way and we should be happy and secure and have pleasure. Isn't that what Hollywood tells us?

But when life doesn't work out, the wind is knocked out of our sails. *What happened?* we think. I thought God loved me. Doesn't He want me to be happy?

Watchman Nee says, "Satan's temptations are not designed primarily to make us do something sinful, but merely to cause us to act in our energy." (Ironically, this quote is from Nee's classic book, *The Normal Christian Life.*)[2]

God's normal is not the world's normal. It is normal for Christians to trust God, to yield to Him, to die to self. But to the world this is absurd; it's unnatural and abnormal.

"The Enemy always tempts us back toward control, to recover and rebuild the false self. We must remember that it is out of love that God thwarts our imposter," says John Eldredge.[3] That's it! We don't trust God – especially when life doesn't work the way we want – because what we want is control.

Control is what Satan tempted Adam and Eve with. "You can be like God. You don't need anyone bossing you around... especially God." And they believed it; and we do, too. But it always backfires. The control we think we want and need just makes us slaves once more to sin (Galatians 5:1).

---

2 Nee, *The Normal Christian Life*, 120.

3 Eldredge, *Wild at Heart,* 111-112.

I'm convinced that the life of faith is mostly about learning to trust God, failing at trusting God, and then allowing Him to pick us back up so we can start to trust Him again. Along the way God does indeed thwart our desire for a normal life. Why? Because He doesn't want for us a normal life. He wants us. He wants our lives wrapped up in His life. Our hearts, our longings, our passions, our dreams. He wants to be our Everything.

2. God Cannot Use Me

Oh, this is a good one. We live in a day of superheroes and superstars, in a world of the haves and the have-nots. In our culture being somebody really matters: being smart, good looking, educated, athletic or musical – the pressure is on to be somebody.

This thinking has seeped into the church as well. The mindset that God only uses the "special" people, those who are ordained or have graduated from seminary, is pervasive. As a result, many are left feeling that they are simply not good enough to be used by God.

The world pushes us to be "somebody" and get recognized for our achievements. But God's Kingdom – a Kingdom made up of the weak, the broken, the pushed-aside, the ordinary – is opposed to the world's obsession with the superstar. Jesus says: "Blessed are the poor in spirit/ the meek/the mournful/the hungry" (see Matthew 5).

There are no superstars in God's Kingdom. In fact, the spiritual superstars of Jesus' day – the Pharisees – were the ones who missed the Kingdom. They thought they were automatically in the Kingdom because of their religious status and position. But they weren't.

So it's a lie to think God will not use us ordinary people. It's also a lie to think God is too busy dealing with big issues like global poverty and AIDS to notice us.

"But what do I have to offer God?" you may ask. The answer is, you. Your life. Come to Him just as you are. That's what He wants.

For years I tried to live out a script I thought others wanted me to live out. I constantly tried to please people, especially people in authority or who I thought were super-spiritual. But I've come to realize that all God wants is for me to be the man He designed. He doesn't want me to try to be somebody other than me. He doesn't want me to compare myself to others or try to be like somebody else. He wants me. And He wants you. So be the you God made you to be.

3. I Don't Have Time For God

As I've mentioned previously, many of my friends who came to the US as refugees or immigrants have said to me, "America is too busy. All you do is work."

I can relate. There was a time when I worked a full-time job with a refugee organization, led a church planting ministry, and did freelance writing on the side. It was nuts! My days and nights were full of ministry, people, writing, and other tasks.

The problem was I wasn't with God. I was too busy running around to do God's work. It took a number of hard circumstances and near-burnout to wake me up.

One of the deadliest and most subtle traps we can fall into is busyness. It's our drug of choice.

The sad truth is, many of us are so busy that we don't have time for relationships – for God and for each other – let alone for reading, for meditating, for taking a walk in the woods. If I understand the journey of faith and what it means to follow Jesus, I think it has more to do with who we are rather than what we do.

Learning to Love and Give

What God really wants for us is to be people who give – who give our lives to Him, who give our lives away to others – and who learn meaning and significance does not come from what we acquire or from our ambitions, but in what we give up and how we sacrifice.

In God's Kingdom everything is abnormal compared to the world's kingdom. Jesus says to be first, we must be last. To gain, we must lose. If we don't die, we can't live. And it's better to give than to get.

The world says the opposite: Grab what you can. It's all about you. You're entitled. Do whatever you feel. Take control of your life.

By God's grace, I am learning to love and to give. I still have so far to go. But I think I'm leaving kindergarten and heading to first grade. At least it's a little progress.

Life is rich when we love and when we give. And when our giving is motivated by what benefits another and not ourselves, we are closer to the heart of God.

Lewis ended his Oxford sermon with a reminder of how we are to live in the midst of war. "If we thought we were building up a heaven on earth, if we looked for something that would turn the present world from a place of pilgrimage into a permanent city satisfying the soul of man, we are disillusioned, and not a moment too soon."[4]

Reflections From the Alley

1. Why do you think God's way of life is considered abnormal in the world's eyes?

2. What lie do you most associate with? (1) Can I trust God? (2) Why would God use me? (3) Do I really have time for God?

Lord, help me to be a person who truly gives – who gives of myself, my time, my resources. Help me live an abnormal life in this world so I can live a Kingdom-life. Show me ways where I'm trying to fit into the world, where I'm self-focused, and how I can grow into the person You want me to become. In Jesus' name, Amen.

---

4 *The Weight of Glory*, 63.

Chapter 12

REFUGE (PART 1): Under His Wings

"God likes pitching a tent with the people of struggle. God is close to
the tears of the poor, and those tears are often a long way from the
centers of power." (Shane Claiborne & Chris Haw)

I believe God wants to transform us into people who deeply trust
Him and who love other people as a result of that trust. He wants us to
be people who provide refuge and shelter and hearth to others.

It's interesting that the word "refugee" is close to the word
"refuge," the giving of shelter and protection. God is often referred to
as our refuge. The Psalms reflect this idea of taking refuge in God,
dwelling in the safety of His presence and protection. David writes,
"The LORD is my rock and my fortress and my deliverer, My God, my
rock, in whom I take refuge" (Psalm 18:2).[1]

But the first time "refuge" is used in the Bible is in relation to a
city that protects or shelters vulnerable people. Can a city be a refuge, a
place of protection and comfort? Think about it: cities have this dark,
almost gruesome connotation about them. We've all seen how movies
and TV shows depict cities as dangerous places. Even the nightly news
of any metropolitan area often focuses on crimes "in the city."

So can a city really be a place of refuge? Well, in God's
perspective and in His plan, yes. And that is precisely how they were
established after the Israelites settled in the Promise Land. Here is the
picture.

God's Refuge Plan

Before the Israelites moved into their new land, God gave Moses a
pep-talk. In Numbers 35, He told Moses to set aside forty-eight cities
for the Levities, the priests of Israel who were called to shepherd and

---

1 NASB.

give pastoral care to the people (35:3-6). This was so they could provide for themselves and their families.

Ligon Duncan, theologian and pastor of First Presbyterian Church of Jackson, Mississippi, gave a compelling sermon on Numbers 35.[2] He said, "God established that there would be pastoral care for all of Israel. All the tribes, spread throughout the land, will have Levities dwelling with the people. This is God's means to carry out pastoral care to His people, including: marriage, death, visiting the sick, and helping people's needs."

The point is, God gave the Levities land and cities, so that they could attend to the poor and the hurting.

Welcomed In

In addition, God set aside six cities where vulnerable people could find refuge and peace. God commanded Moses:

"Speak to the sons of Israel and say to them, 'When you cross the Jordan into the land of Canaan, then you shall select for yourselves cities to be your cities of refuge, that the manslayer who has killed any person unintentionally may flee there. The cities shall be to you as a refuge from the avenger, so that the manslayer will not die until he stands before the congregation for trial. The cities which you are to give shall be your six cities of refuge'" (35:10-13).[3]

God made it possible for people to find refuge within these six, set-apart cities. There the Levitical priests would counsel with those who had been torn from their family and friends, and offer them comfort and hope. But these cities were not only for displaced Israelites; they were also for aliens and sojourners.

"These six cities shall be for refuge for the sons of Israel, and for the alien and for the sojourner among them; that anyone who kills a person unintentionally may flee there" (35:15).[4] Here we see that even

---

2 Duncan, "Cities of Refuges."

3 NASB.

4 NASB.

aliens (non-Jews) or sojourners (those passing through) were welcomed in and given pastoral care.

A Good Reminder

This passage is a good reminder of how God provides refuge and help to people who are struggling, to the world's poor and oppressed. Sam, my friend who lived for ten years in a Thai refugee camp, is a living example of someone who has experienced God's refuge and provisions in miraculous ways. Sam is Karen-Burmese, an ethnic group that has been brutally persecuted by Burma's military government.

"The Karen people are in danger of ethnic cleansing," said Sam. "The Burmese government, village by village, is attempting to wipe out this people group."

Thankfully, Sam escaped to Thailand, and eventually was resettled in America as a refugee. He now is helping other Burmese refugees adjust to the joys and challenges of American life.

Like the Levites, we too are called to be a refuge to people in need in our cities: offering them guidance, a listening ear, a hot meal, and the strength to go another day – in a word, to practice hospitality. This is God's will (His Kingdom) being done on earth. God is close to displaced people. He always has been.

Jesus knew displacement, having to flee for His life under the cover of night to Egypt. Abraham was displaced, called out of his country to follow God to an unknown place. David was displaced, being forced to hide out in caves and the desert because of Saul's jealous rage. For four hundred long years, God's people lived in displacement in Egypt under the tyranny of the mightiest nation in the world at that time.

Jesus Is ...

And so, like these Karen refugees in Thailand, we hold on, waiting and hoping to finally be resettled in our permanent residence – to be joined with God and His family once and for all. In the meantime, just as God provides for us, cares for us, and shelters us, we too are called to do the same for others. We are to be a *refuge* to a world of oppression, to the have-nots, and for those who just don't fit in.

Jesus is our City of Refuge where the hurting, the rejected, the broken, and the poor of this world can go and find mercy and comfort.

Jesus is our warmth on a cold day and our shade on a hot day. Jesus is our protection from the harshness of the world. He is hearth. And in His presence we find all the refuge and shelter we need. Jesus will...

> *Cover you with his feathers,*
> *and under his wings you will find refuge*
> (Psalm 91:4)

Reflections From the Alley

1. How has God been a refuge and shelter in your life?

2. Read Psalm 91. What do you observe?

Lord, I look for refuge and comfort in You. I know I cannot make it by myself. Open my eyes to the needs of people around me. Help me to pray for and care for those who are suffering in the world. Give me Your eyes and Your compassion for them. In Jesus name, Amen.

Chapter 13

REFUGE (PART 2): The Story of Tham Hin

"Sir, we are not journalists. We just want to see the people."

A few years back, I had one of the most impactful experiences of my life. My wife and I had an opportunity to visit Thailand, spending the majority of our trip in Bangkok, where our good friend, Jim, lived and worked as an English teacher.

At that time, I worked with a lot of Burmese refugees in Chicago who once lived in refugee camps in Thailand. And so we planned to visit one of those camps. Tham Hin is located southwest of Bangkok and runs closely parallel to the Burmese border. We thought we had clearance to go to the camp, but we soon found out it would be a little harder than we thought.

Shortly after we arrived in Bangkok, we attempted to contact the UNCHR[1] to get permission to go to Tham Him. But they bounced us over to the OPE, better known as the Ministry of Interior of Thailand. They were of no help. Our letter of intent and copies of our passports which we faxed weeks prior did nothing for our cause. They denied us permission to go the camp, stating that we didn't have a valid enough reason.

The Risk

We decided to take a risk and go to the camp anyway. Although a few people had warned us not to go to the border of Burma, a country riddled with conflict and violence, we knew God had put it on our hearts to go.

My Karen-Burmese friend who came as a refugee to Chicago had lived in Tham Hin for ten years. So I called him from Bangkok and asked for his advice. He told me we should visit the camp.

---

1 UNCHR stands for United Nations High Commissioner for Refugees. For more information, check out: http://www.unhcr.org/cgi-bin/texis/vtx/home.

On a Sunday afternoon, we made our way through the pouring rain and heavy traffic of Bangkok to the bus station. There we boarded a bus headed for Ratchaburi, the region of Thailand where Tham Hin is located. We knew how to get to Ratchaburi but had no idea how to get to the camp from there. This was truly a faith journey.

When we arrived in Ratchaburi, we met up with a young couple who had started up a new ministry in the area. They loved the idea of going to the camp and decided to accompany us.

The next day, we found out no bus would travel that far west to the border where the camp was located. So we ended up hiring a driver and a van – which proved to be the only way to get to the camp. From there, it was an adventure through the wilderness of Thailand. The region was beautiful and reminded me of the opening scenes of the old TV show *M*A*S*H*.

Lush banana trees lined the road. Rice fields stretched as far as the eye could see. We saw pineapple trees, wild monkeys, and green mountains in the distant. It was breathtaking. Our Thai friends pointed west and said, "There is Burma, just over those mountains."

We were so close. I thought, *Here I am in this Eden-like land, surrounded by beauty, and yet there is so much violence and oppression and poverty just over those mountains.*

Temporary Shelter

Our driver eventually got us to the camp after traversing steep, uphill dirt roads and crossing small rivers that formed as a result of the rainy season. As we entered the camp, we were greeted with a sign that read, "Tham Hin Temporary Shelter" in both Thai and English, along with Thai soldiers with big guns (and I don't mean muscles).

We got out of the van and our translator spoke with a guard, attempting to plead our case and get us inside the camp. The guards brought over another man, a stout army official who wore camouflage and dark sun glasses. We learned he was the director.

As our translator spoke to the director in Thai, and made hand motions which included pointing to me, I could tell by his expression he wasn't going to let us in. "He's not going to let us go inside the camp," the translator confirmed.

My Nehemiah Prayer

I shot up a prayer, like Nehemiah did when he approached the king for permission to go back to Jerusalem. Then I said through our translator to the camp director, "Sir, we are not journalists. We just want to see the people." The director's body language changed. He pointed toward the camp and said something in Thai. Our translator said, "We can see the camp but we cannot go inside." God heard my prayer. The only condition was we could not take any photos.

We made our way up a steep path to the top of a hill and entered a wooded picnic-like area. The area served as a station where the refugees would come for their interviews to get into the camp, receive a medical exam, and exited the camp to be resettled in a different country.

From that hill, I saw a sight I will never forget.

There beneath us, only a couple hundred yards away, was the refugee camp. A tall, wooden fence surrounded the perimeter of the camp. Just past the fence were hundreds of houses. They were small, square-looking wooden structures, all squished together. We learned from the Thai director that about 10,000 Karen refugees were crammed together in Tham Hin camp, which looked about the size of a couple of football fields.[2]

We could hear in the distance a megaphone of some sort. It was a call for families to come get their rations of food – rations, we learned, which were to last for a week. Inside this city of refuge, children could go to school and learn English and learn about Western culture. Outside aid organizations would come in and teach English, nutrition, hygiene, as well as give medical attention, and other social services.

We learned that the majority of refugees in the camp waited tirelessly for the day when they were called up to the interview station to hear the good news of their acceptance to a new country, specifically America or Canada.

---

2 The Karen people are an ethnic minority group in Burma located in southeastern Burma. They have been severely persecuted by the Burmese government, forcing them to flee into Thailand. For more information, check out this webpage: http://karennews.org/tag/refugees/.

People of Struggle

As I looked to the west past the mountains, I couldn't help but think about all of the pain and suffering inflicted on these people in one of the most dangerous countries in the world. And I thought about the families I know back in Chicago who lived here for ten years or longer.

I thought of my very first Burmese family, a Karen family of seven from this same camp, who arrived at O'Hare Airport on a snowy day in March with one suitcase and sandals on their feet, and no jackets.

I thought about God and how He is close to the oppressed and alien, and that He, as Shane Claiborne said, pitches His tent with the "people of struggle."[3] I couldn't help but think all of all I have back in America and how far removed I am from anything like this. And how far removed these refugees are from places like Wall Street or Capitol Hill or Michigan Avenue in Chicago.

"And I wondered if the Kingdom of God looks more like this refugee camp ..."

And I wondered if the Kingdom of God looks more like this refugee camp, a place where people are in desperation, holding on to the hope that one day life will be better and they will, once again, have a place to call home.

I'll never forget the sight of Tham Hin. The smells, the feeling, the sounds of children below, some playing, some crying, the eerie-looking plot just outside of the camp used as a cemetery. Tham Hin will forever be etched in my memory.

The Cover of Night

These Karen refugees did not flee their country because of an accidental murder. They fled because they had to. They fled under the cover of night, with their children, through the jungles of Burma until they crossed into Thailand. Once in Thailand, they were placed in a

---

3 Claiborne and Haw, *Jesus for President*, 35.

temporary shelter, a city of refuge, where they were protected from the militia and those who seek to destroy them.

These shelters, however, are far from glamorous.

Because of overcrowding and a lack of medical provisions, sickness and disease are rampant. Sometimes authorities have to quarantine the whole camp and not let anyone in from outside because diseases spread so rapidly. Some don't make it out of the camp; others, like my friends in Chicago, do.

The word "poor" is used 176 times in the Bible.[4] It's very clear from Scripture that God's heart is for the poor. And He's constantly reminding His people to care about and provide for the poor. In fact, you could almost argue God seems to favor the poor. "He raises the poor from the dust and lifts the needy from the ash heap; he seats them with princes and has them inherit a throne of honor" (1 Samuel 2:8).

We, therefore, living in one of the richest countries in the world, need to take this very seriously. If God's heart is for the poor, the oppressed, the stranger, and the marginalized, then so must our hearts. Tham Hin is just one place amid thousands around the world where people suffer.

To bless another is to take action. It's easy to watch the news or hear the stories of people out there but not let their plight touch our hearts. We are called to care, to be the hands and feet of Jesus to a world in need. We can give and bless because we have *something* to give and bless people with – the love of Jesus. Let us not sit around hoarding the blessing and live passive and clueless lives. Let's take what we have and give it away to people in need!

---

4 This number is based on the NIV translation.

Reflections From the Alley

1. Consider praying about a particular displaced/refugee group in the world. It could be the Karen people, or Iraqi refugees, or refugees from Nepal or Somali or Sudan. Find out if there are any refugee groups who have resettled in your area. Get to know about them and get involved somehow.

Consider these statistics:[5]

- There are approximately 43 million refugees worldwide.
- 41% of refugees are under the age of 18, and 11% are under 5.
- Approximately 10.5 million people are in refugee camps.
- Every year on October 1st, the President determines how many refugees will enter the U.S. the following year.
- Between 2010 and 2011, about 80 million refugees were resettled to America, which is the maximum amount the U.S. will accept.
- Only 42% of adults polled by the UNCHR knew that a refugee is a person who is forced to leave his or her home country.
- The average stay in a refugee camp is 17 years.
- The world's largest refugee camp – located in Kenya – is full.
- The State Department estimates about 4 million Iraqis have been displaced.
- Since the start of the Iraq war, the State Department has sent tens of thousands of Iraqi refugees to metro Detroit. The government resettled 2,744 people — mainly Iraqis — to the Detroit area from June 25, 2008, to June 24, 2009.
- In 2011, 41,000 people were displaced in Sudan due to the conflict between North and South Sudan.

---

5 These statistics are from World Relief Chicago, presented at World Refugee Day, June 17, 2011, and from the Global Trends Report from the UNHCR. For more information, check out: www.youtube.com/watch?v=g3WTea7yGZg.

HOMECOMING

SECTION THREE

SECTION 3

HOMECOMING

"Hope begins in the dark, the stubborn hope that if you just show up and try to do the right thing, the dawn will come. You wait and watch and work: You don't give up." (Anne Lamott)

Homecoming: *noun*
1. a coming to or returning home.

I am amazed at how hopeful displaced people are. Many of the refugees I know – like my friend, Fiko – still find the strength to keep going and believe life will get better, in spite of all the loss and hardship and pain they have endured. Many have told me it was their dream to come to America, to live in a land of freedom, and they never lost hope of seeing their dream come to fruition.

Hope is a powerful thing. It gets us up in the morning. It keeps us moving forward. Within every human being is the capacity to hope, to believe there is more to life than what is seen – that we are made for something more, something bigger.

Hope moves us toward our ultimate place. It is where longing and realization finally kiss. That kiss is called Homecoming.

I believe there are three aspects of Homecoming:

- *Sentness* – This is an understanding that God has a plan for us because we are to be a sent people, called to carry out His purposes.
- *Meaningful Work* – In order to carry out God's purposes, our work must be focused on a cause higher than ourselves.
- *Longing* – The only way our work is meaningful is by believing and hoping in what is to come (Heaven) and pursuing that goal with all our hearts.

In the following chapters, I will flesh out these three aspects in more detail. But first, I'd like to introduce you to a friend of mine.

His name is Carl Johnson. He's an artist, a poet, and the founder of Saint-Creative, a print, web, and branding organization. And he knows all about what it means to be sent, to engage in meaningful work, and to long for his permanent residency.[1]

Called To Create (Sentness)

In 2010, Carl was laid off from his job, a media company in the Detroit area. But amid one of the toughest recessions of all time, in one of the toughest metropolitan areas in the U.S., Carl felt God leading him to step out in faith and do what seemed impossible. He started his own business.

"I did it out of necessity. Really, God positioned and ordained me for this," Carl said. "The idea God gave me was to find the extraordinary in the ordinary. Really, restlessness drives me continually, which is a blessing and a curse. Restlessness is a divine discontent about things. And it makes you keep going in your mission."

Carl clearly sees himself as sent by God. "I've never really fit in. I've always adhered to the term 'counter-cultural.' I am destined to be sent toward seasoning our culture through art – using art as an expression. This is the seasoning and salt aspect Jesus talks about." But to get to this point, Carl endured a lot.

After he lost his job, he lost his house. As a result, he and his wife and two small children moved into his parents' house. But throughout, Carl didn't lose hope. In fact, it made him stronger and more willing to take risks.

"A lot of the feelings I had and the restlessness led me to create art," Carl said. Enter Saint Creative, a non-profit organization that has inspired many people, and a magazine called *Greater Than*, which focuses on shaping culture through art, music, poetry, and music

---

1 To learn more about Saint-Creative, check out www.saint-creative.com.

110

reviews.[2] Both are intended as ways to create dialogue with people about Christ.

"We're all searchers," Carl mentioned. "It's OK if it's not blatant like Christian T-shirts. I think Christ is mysterious. Let's let people discover this themselves. One of the purposes of art is to create dialogue. Really, it's conversation that we're really interested in at the end of the day. This is what we want. Think about it: Would you rather tell people about Jesus or talk about Him with them?"

Carl sees himself as the "saint" of creativity. "I've always been interested in imagination and inspiration. I've been enchanted by the Catholic emphasis on the saints. And I thought, 'Wow, who is the saint of creativity and imagination?' So my tagline for my company is the saint of inspired work and imagination."

To Serve and Be Creative (Meaningful Work)

Carl sees his work as meaningful. His work – whether it's a banner for a major company, business cards, poetry for his magazine or a music review – fulfills him. But it doesn't fulfill him in an egotistical way, or in a way that drives him toward financial prosperity.

"From a personal standpoint," Carl said, "the point of Saint Creative is to serve and be creative. Serving others is lost art form in the church world. From a corporate stand point, Saint Creative exists to create beautiful, intentional, memorable, effective, remarkable work for our clients."

Carl also sees his work as a way to bless his clients by praying for them. "I want them to succeed. I want them to advance in their field."

I've experienced this firsthand with Carl, when he helped me with some design work for promoting my ministry, and worked to make my website and blog what they are today.[3]

---

2 Check out www.greaterthanmag.com.

3 www.reflectionsfromthealley.org.

A Rock Opera (Longing)

When I asked Carl what he wants his legacy to be, he didn't hesitate in his response. "I want people to say, 'Dude, this guy was doing art for Christ for his whole life. He kept his hand on the plow.' We're not ultimately going to find fulfillment and satisfaction here in this world. You have to realize there's more."

This is the essence of Homecoming, the realization that there is more. But it's a realization coupled with a purposeful life – a life lived with intention, with risk, with a sense of urgency. For Carl, it's a life of inspiration. "The most fascinating thing in Scripture is when God breathed His life – His wind – inside of us. If we have this inside of us, you can tap into that divine breath. You are touching into God's creativity. And in turn, we can inspire others with the Divine Breath."

Carl believes deeply that we are called to inspire. Whether it's in music, poetry, business, or brewing coffee, they are all just tributaries for God to use to bring inspiration. "If you're not living an inspired life, you're not really living. Can you imagine living uninspired? Wouldn't that be depressing?"

Consider this music review Carl wrote for *Greater Than* about the alternative band The Violet Burning and their album, *The Story of Our Lives*:

> Longing is a powerful emotion expressed through music. Two things that the Violet Burning long for are heart and home. It's evident in all their albums actually, and equally strong here. The main character, who could be me or you, is on a search and a journey. (Being a concept album, there has to be an element of journey). He's looking for meaning, worth and home in the culture and times that he finds himself in. I think the Violet Burning are very close to finding home.

> It's kind of a beautiful journey.

> Which leads me to the next item of discussion.

> The Violet Burning have reinforced a critical and essential goal for any Christian making art: simply put, to help bring beauty to the ruin.

Often times our lives are this strange mixture of beauty and ruin. We must be making beautiful things that contrast the darkness around us.

And Carl is doing that: making things beautiful in contrast to the darkness surrounding us.

My hope for this section, then, is to help you see how you can make your life – amid all of the darkness and ruin – beautiful and meaningful. To do so requires us to yearn for that which awaits us – our Homecoming.

Paul said it this way: "But one thing I do: Forgetting what lies behind and straining toward what is ahead, I press on toward the goal to win the prize for which God has called me heavenward in Christ Jesus" (Philippians 3:13-14).

So let us move forward with purpose and meaning, believing we are sent by God to be engaged in meaningful work, as we keep our longing for home ever before us.

"Psalm 37 is one of my favorite Scriptures," Carl mentioned. "It says the steps of a righteous man are orchestrated by the Lord. God's making a musical piece with our lives. A symphony or piece of music. Hopefully mine will be a rock opera!"

Chapter 14

MOVEMENT: *Go with God*

"'They say Aslan is on the move - perhaps has already landed.'
And now a very curious thing happened. None of the children knew
who Aslan was any more than you do; but the moment the Beaver had
spoken these words everyone felt quite different."
(C.S. Lewis, *The Lion, The Witch, and The Wardrobe*)

Faith moves us forward. It's the idea of going with God who is constantly on the move. And He wants us to join in. I learned this principle – go with God – from a dear lady who I had the privilege of knowing a couple of years.

I believe she was sent by God to teach me many things. But there is one thing she taught me in particular ...

In a stunningly beautiful area of America – known as the Appalachians – lies a mountain range stretching from Mississippi to southern New York. From the 1930s through the 1950s, thousands of "mountain people" – mostly from West Virginia, North Carolina, and Tennessee – left their rural homes and migrated north to the industrial cities of Chicago, Detroit, and Akron, Ohio. The movement was known as the Hillbilly Highway.[1]

A young girl named Katie Torres, along with her mother, were among these migrants.

I met Katie in inner-city Chicago through another pastor who worked with her and her family. For a couple of years, in fact, some people from our church and I did a Bible study every week in Katie's apartment.

---

1 For more information on this, check out this article: http://www.arc.gov/
appalachian_region/TheAppalachianRegion.asp.

Transformation

Katie had lived a hard life. At a young age, her mother moved her to the big city from Appalachian North Carolina. She faced hard times on the streets: fighting poverty, getting caught up in prostitution, drugs, you name it. But when she came to Jesus later in life, a major transformation took place. She sobered up, remarried, and sought to raise her daughter in the ways of the Lord.

God's light shone brightly in her; she was always talking about His grace and her longing for heaven. She didn't hide the fact that she was tough; she was who she was - using choice words sometimes, smoking a lot, eating badly. But she sure did love Jesus and her family, especially her grandkids whom she practically raised. She created a hearth for her family, a place of hospitality and love.

Her one motto, something she would say to me every time I would get ready to leave her home, was, "Go with God." Three simple words. But words full of depth and impact. Words Katie both said and lived.

In the fall of 2008, Katie Torres passed away after a long battle with diabetes and cancer. It was a huge loss – especially to her daughter and grandkids. I had the honor of facilitating her funeral. My eulogy was entitled, "Go with God." It was by far the most unique funeral I have ever done.

The audience included gang bangers, neighborhood friends, young and old, all coming to pay tribute to this dear lady who touched so many lives. And they all knew Katie's famous phrase, "go with God." On that day, we had a church service – and Katie was preaching even though she was with Jesus. Really, her life was the message.

People of Movement

Just as Katie and thousands of Appalachians moved from their rural homes up north in search for work, so we too, the displaced followers of Christ, are always on the move.

Displacement is both living in an unnatural environment and the act of uniform movement. To be displaced means to be moving. And if you take a good look at Scripture, and a good look at history, you will see God's people are invariably a people of movement.

Abraham was a man on the move. He was called to leave behind all the comforts of home, go to places he knew nothing about, and live in tents.

David was on the move from Saul's seething jealousy. He hid in caves, in the desert, in cities. But wherever David went, God moved with him, sustaining and guiding him. And it was in his flight he penned some of the most beautiful poetry the world has ever known – the Psalms.

Esther, too, was so moved by compassion for her people that she willingly married the King of Persia, Xerxes, and thus thwarted the genocide of the Jewish people in her day. Esther purposefully moved herself into a dangerous position for the sake of others, becoming their advocate by sacrificing herself.

And Jesus was always on the move. He and His parents were forced to flee Herod's wrath, taking refuge in Egypt. His entire earthly ministry was one of constantly going from place to place.

God on the Move

Each of these people were displaced. They found themselves in situations that caused them to deeply trust in God and move in the direction He willed. They were willing to go with God.

To be displaced, then, not only means living in an unfamiliar environment, but also being willing to be on the move. The book of Hebrews captures this. "By faith Abraham, when called to go to a place he would later receive as his inheritance, obeyed and went, even though he did not know where he was going. By faith he made his home in the Promised Land like a stranger in a foreign country; he lived in tents, as did Isaac and Jacob, who were heirs with him of the same promise. For he was looking forward to the city with foundations, whose architect and builder is God" (11:8-10).

"The Christian optimism," G.K. Chesterton said, "is based on the fact that we do not fit in to the world ... I knew now why grass had always seemed to me as queer as the green beard of a giant, and why I could feel homesick at home."[2] How can we feel at home if we don't fit in and are called to be on the move?

Even in Detroit, a city that is the poster child for urban blight and our bad economy, I see God on the move. And I see people – creative and brilliant and courageous people – moving into the city, restoring and renovating old downtown buildings, planting urban gardens, and working toward sustainable transformation.

Willingness

The truth is, God is at work. And He calls us to join Him. To do so requires the willingness to trust Him, even when it doesn't make sense.

I remember vividly, while at a conference in Atlanta, when the Lord called my wife and me to move out of our comfortable, middle-class suburb and live and work in the inner city.

It was both exciting and scary. Exciting because my wife and I knew God was calling us to the city; scary because we had no idea what to do or how we would make it financially. (I had to leave a good job with security and benefits.)

But when God calls you, He will make it very clear, placing things in your life to remind you that He is in this. For me, one of those reminders was this poem:

I said: "Let me walk in the field."
God said: "Nay, walk in the town."
I said: "There are no flowers there."
He said: "No flowers, but a crown."
I said: "But the sky is black,
There is nothing but noise and din."
But He wept as He sent me back,
"There is more," he said, "there is sin."
I said: "But the air is thick,
And fog is veiling the sun."
He answered: "Yet souls are sick,
And souls in the dark undone."

---

2 Chesterton, *Orthodoxy*, 80.

I said: "I shall miss the light,
And friends will miss me, they say."
He answered me: "Choose tonight
If I am to miss you, or they."
I pleaded for time to be given.
He said: "Is it hard to decide?
It will not seem hard in Heaven
To have followed the steps of your Guide."
I cast one look at the fields,
Then set my face to the town.
He said, "My child, do you yield?
Will you leave the flowers for the crown?"
Then into His hand went mine,
And into my heart came He;
And I walk in a light Divine
The streets I had feared to see.[3]

Those words were exactly what I needed to hear. The sacrifice – leaving a good job and a beautiful home – paled in comparison to the broken and bruised people of the inner city.

"Will you leave the flowers for the crown?" McDonald beckons. Will you seek God's best and do what He has called you to do? Or will you let fear or the what-ifs get in the way?

As Eugene Peterson understood it, "The streets and fields, the homes and markets of the world, are an art gallery displaying not culture, but new creations in Christ."[4] The "streets" is where God sent me. And when I got there, I met a treasure: Katie Torres.

Katie's life did not start out well. It actually took many years, and many bad choices, before she gave her life to Jesus and started to live right. But she definitely finished well. She wanted to experience God's best and she saw herself as sent by God to fulfill His purposes.

Let us not squander the time and life God has given us. Let us live sent-lives and be willing to go where He calls.

---

3 George MacDonald, found on "Wanderings and Wonderings: http://amishwolf.blogspot.com/2008/03/streets-i-feared-to-see.html.

4 Peterson, *The Contemplative Pastor*, 6.

In whatever you do and wherever you are called – Go with God.

Reflections From the Alley

1. In what way right now do you think God wants you to go with Him? What does it mean for you to go with God?

2. How has God sent you? Where do you sense He is sending you now?

Lord, help me to be willing to go and do whatever You ask of me. I want to live my life as one being sent, as one who moves according to Your plan. Help me be willing to face my fears, my what-ifs, and trust You no matter what. In Jesus' name, Amen.

Chapter 15

PURSUIT: The Quest Before Us

"We pursue God because, and only because, He has first put an urge within us that spurs us to the pursuit." (A.W. Tozer)

If you grew up in the 1990s, you may remember one of the greatest gifts ever bestowed during that decade – Nintendo. I got my first box, I think, in 1990 or 1991. And my favorite game, a game I kept going back to over and over, was *The Legend of Zelda*.

This game is a mixture of action, fantasy, adventure, and mystery. The protagonist, Link, is on a mission to save the elf-princess, Zelda. To get to her, Link has to make it through different levels full of dungeons, forests, towns, and labyrinths. The main goal, of course, was to rescue Zelda. But the point of the game was not so much to get through the levels quickly, or to destroy all the enemies and rescue the princess, but to explore new areas, solve puzzles, and look for weapons and maps. It was the pursuit, the quest along the way, which made this game so rich.

> "Jesus places us in new areas and new levels that require us to trust Him and to continue moving forward."

To be honest, I don't even remember if I ever rescued poor, desolate Princess Zelda. My favorite part of the game was exploring new areas and figuring out how to get to the next one. This, I think, is a good picture of faith in displacement.

New Levels

Jesus places us in new areas and takes us to new levels that require us to trust Him and to continue moving forward. And often where we grow in Him the most are the hardest places, or the places we've never been before. As Link gets closer to his ultimate goal, rescuing the princess, the more difficult the levels become. His enemies come after him with more intensity.

Similarly, for Pilgrim, the main character of John Bunyan's classic, *The Pilgrim's Progress*, the closer he got to the Celestial City the more obstacles he faced. "It is when heaven's heights are in full view that the gates of hell are the most persistent and full of deadly peril."[1]

This is true for our lives as well. The more we pursue Christ and seek to live our lives for Him on this earth, the more the kingdom of darkness will come against us. If darkness wasn't against us, would we really trust God and seek after Him?

The point of both *The Legend of Zelda* and *Pilgrim's Progress* is to depict a journey, a pursuit, a quest for adventure and beauty and rescue. The same can be said of our faith pursuit.

Let People See Your Pursuit

As I've mentioned, part of my pursuit of God has been working with refugees from all over the world, listening to their stories, attempting to mend their wounds, and seeing God work in their lives. This is where God has *sent* me.

I get various opinions and facial expressions when I tell people that I work with Muslim immigrants and refugees. Some have asked me why I work with *those* people. *How do you even reach out to them? They're terrorists!* It seems to me that some Christians see Muslims like the Jews saw the Samaritans in Jesus' day – people who don't deserve God's love. I get it. There is a lot of fear and misunderstanding when it comes to Islam, and of course 9/11 pushed a lot of people over the edge.

In addition, there are a lot of opinions and approaches Christians use to reach out to Muslims, especially where I live in Dearborn, which is one the largest concentration of Arabs outside of the Middle East. There are those who are well-versed in the religion of Islam and use the Qur'an (Islam's holy book) to witness about Jesus and the Christian faith. There are others who use more of an apologetic approach, trying to convince and persuade Muslims to believe in Christianity.

---

1 Cowman, *Streams in the Desert,* 100.

I honestly think the best way to reach out to Muslims (or any lost person, for that matter) is by letting them see you are close to God. I once heard Dwight Robertson, president of Kingdom Building Ministries say, years ago, "The greatest gift we can give the world is our intimacy with God."

That stuck with me and I believe it is true.

What people need to see are believers who are really pursuing God and who care about people, even people who are different from them and speak different languages or believe in other religions. Let people see your pursuit. Let them see you are on a journey and that you don't have it all figured out. Let them see that your life is hard at times and you often don't feel like you fit in.

Pursuing God as He Pursues Us

Why? Because God's family is comprised of people who don't fit in. His family is for those kids who were picked last on those dreaded days at recess, and for those who give up so much of what the world has to offer in favor of a better world to come. His family is for those who can't make it on their own but refuse to give up.

I have learned this from the Iraqi people I've worked with in Chicago and now in Detroit. Many of my clients had high-paid professional jobs in Iraq. When they came to America, they had to start all over, often working at low-paying labor jobs. They so badly want to fit in to American culture, get good jobs right away, send their children to the best schools, and live in nice apartments or buy a house. Unfortunately, this is far from reality, especially in light of our economic recession.

But they don't give up. They keep pursuing the better life, knowing that life in America, as hard as it is for them, far outweighs life in Iraq where they'd face hopelessness and perhaps even death. I've told some of my clients not to think of me as their teacher. They are my teachers.

Citizenship

Many of the Iraqis I know are so courageous, so grateful to be alive, and so hopeful for their futures.

A few months back, one Iraqi refugee told me how he was captured by a group of people in Baghdad, interrogated, and beaten. They were planning to kill him unless his family paid a large sum of money for his ransom, which they did. He said, "I think God must love me very much because I am here now and not dead."

This young man is optimistic about his life in America, and although he is Muslim, he is open to Jesus and reads the Bible regularly. I am confident God is at work in his life, pursuing and loving him.

The other day I helped a different Iraqi man study for his citizenship test while sitting in Tim Horton's coffee shop. As I finished the last few questions – questions pertaining to federal laws and the rights of Americans – my friend said, "I love America. It's the best country." My friend believes it was God who sent him here. And he doesn't take that for granted.

He works hard at his job, supports his wife who is in school, and studied vigorously for his interview so he can become a citizen.

Paul says we are citizens of heaven and should eagerly wait for our Savior (Philippians 3:20). If this is true, should we not work as hard at our faith just as my friend did to become a citizen of America? Isn't our heavenly citizenship more worthy than our any allegiance to our country?

Understanding What Awaits Us

We should long for our heavenly citizenship while we trudge through the alleys of life. It's this longing, I believe, which makes our faith strong and our witness attractive. Just like Link in *The Legend of Zelda*, our pursuit is filled with adventure and danger. Life this side of heaven is a war zone. And as such, we need to be prepared for battle, keeping our feet on the narrow path, believing we are sent to carry out God's purposes, and never giving up the pursuit.

Understanding what awaits us – our homecoming – is crucial if we are to live effectively and meaningfully in displacement. It will require us to pursue God with everything we've got, trusting Him as He leads us to unknown places and new levels. We also need to allow God to pursue us, to show us new things, to help us see people and circumstances the way He does.

We are the characters in His story. He is the Author. We need to let Him develop the plot, and let Him write the story of our lives. For our part, we must pursue Him just as He pursues us.

As good and rich as life can be in the here and now, it can never replace what lies ahead – our true residency with God. As much as my Iraqi friend loves America, he'll never stop loving his homeland, and especially, his family there. "When I become a citizen," he told me, "I have to visit Iraq. I must see my mother." I saw the longing in his eyes.

Will others see a longing for our heavenly home in our eyes?

Reflections From The Alley

1. Why is it the closer we get to God the more obstacles and challenges come our way? Is this true for your life?

2. What "level" do you feel that God is leading you to?

Thank You, Lord, for always pursuing me. You've never given up on me. Help me to be open to You leading me to new levels in my life. Help me to be courageous and trusting and willing to see things as You do. Help me to never stop pursuing You as long as I live. In Jesus' name, Amen.

Chapter 16

PURPOSE: *What Hagar Can Teach Us*

"Conversion is not the smooth, easy-going process some men seem to think… It is wounding work, of course, this breaking of the hearts, but without wounding there is no saving." (John Bunyan)

One day I was praying, feeling overwhelmed with the amount of need I see in my community. God led me to a passage in Genesis that completely rattled me. It's the story of Hagar, the Egyptian maidservant of Abraham's wife, Sarah. As I read this story and prayed, the Lord spoke to my heart and reminded me that there are many in my community like Hagar: they've been pushed aside, sent away, and who long for a place to call home.

The story of Hagar is an interesting one. God appeared to Abraham and told him that he would have a son and that his son's descendants would be as numerous as the stars (Genesis 15). Abraham believed God. In return, He "credited [his faith] to him as righteousness" (15:6, brackets mine). I'm sure Abraham went home to his wife, Sarah, beaming: "We're going to have a baby! Isn't that wonderful?"

I imagine this must have been quite a shock to Sarah. "Um, did God forget how old we are? We are well past the childbearing season of our lives. What about our plans to move to Phoenix?" Nevertheless, the couple believed God and trusted in His promise.

Isn't it exciting when the Lord reveals something to us and answers our prayers? At those moments, it's as if everything in the world is as it should be. But those moments don't seem to last long or work out the way we think they should.

"Helping" God Out

For Abraham and Sarah, things weren't moving fast enough. Sarah was still not pregnant. So she took matters into her own hands and convinced her husband to marry and sleep with Hagar, Sarah's servant. Sure enough, Hagar got pregnant and Ishmael was born.

Now stop right there, lest we be too harsh on Sarah. Don't we do the same thing? God reveals something to us, or answers that prayer we've been praying forever about. We get excited. *God still loves me and hears my prayers!* But then something happens: Things don't move as fast as we'd like. The job we prayed about, felt a peace about, and were interviewed for, goes to someone else. Our spouse isn't changing for the better fast enough. The phone conversation with a distant parent didn't go the way we'd hoped – we're still distant.

And so we decide to help God out, as if to think this will speed up us getting what we want. Life isn't working out the way we felt God said it would be. And so we take over. We take control.

Abraham is rejoicing he will have a son; Sarah is fuming. The account says, "She began to despise her mistress" (16:4). Hello! Well of course she did. The plan backfired, because it wasn't God's plan. His plan, His promise, was that Abraham and Sarah *together* would have a son.

God still brought His good out of their disobedience. No child is an accident. God had a plan for Hagar and for Ishmael. But now there was tension, jealousy, and envy – all those nasty sins that rear their ugly heads when we trust in our own abilities and strength rather than God's.

Rejection

Fast forward thirteen years. God's promise was fulfilled: Sarah got pregnant and had a son with Abraham. They named him Isaac. He was to be the seed of the nation of Israel, just as God planned. The family had to celebrate – and in their culture that meant one thing: a feast.

The next scene gets a little tense. Ishmael began to mock Isaac (Genesis 21:9). We're not sure what Ishmael did exactly. All we're told is he mocked or poked fun at Isaac, possibly out of jealousy. But it was the final straw for Sarah and she wanted them to leave and never come back. She convinced Abraham to "get rid of that slave woman and her son" (21:10).

Poor ol' Abe. He was torn. Ishmael was also his son, but Sarah was unhappy. So he sent Hagar and Ishmael away with only a skin of water and some food.

Modern-Day Hagars

Many of the refugees and immigrants I work with are from Iraq. Almost all of them have horrific stories of being threatened, followed by unmarked cars, or having had family members killed. They have literarily been pushed aside and forced to flee their country out of sheer terror. And so they leave – they take a bus or a car, navigating their way through all the Iraqi check points, finally arriving at their destination in Jordan, Syria, Turkey or Lebanon.

When they arrive, they are usually treated as outcasts. Many of them cannot work. In Syria, for example, Iraqi refugees are not able to get work visas and are forced to live off of their savings or have extended family members wire money from Iraq so they can make ends meet.

I saw this firsthand when my wife and I went to Amman, Jordan, in 2008. We visited some Iraqi refugees who were waiting to be placed in the United States. Their living conditions, compared to the typical Jordanian, were anything but desirable. Their street was rundown, dusty, and away from the restaurants and cafes and malls so prevalent in Amman. As we walked up their staircase, handrails were missing and the building was in need of some maintenance. Their apartment was modest and their furniture sparse.

They were living as strangers and exiles in a neighboring country where the same language is spoken.

The younger sister of the family went to school and the older one took care of her. She worked occasionally at a hair salon where she made a little bit of cash. But it was by no means a living.

Honor and Shame

People from the Middle East live by honor and shame. In the West, we often measure a person's standing in the community by what they do (such as jobs, levels of income, and education). This is not the case in the Middle East, where your worth as a person depends a lot on what kind of family you are from.

For Hagar to be kicked out of Abraham's family was the utmost form of rejection. There was no greater shame. What was she to do now? She was alone, abandoned, depressed. There was no more water, no more food. Hagar was forced to place her son under some bushes, unwilling to watch him die of starvation and dehydration. But then God showed up as He usually does when we are at the end of ourselves.

"God heard the boy crying, and the angel of God called to Hagar from heaven and said to her, 'What is the matter, Hagar? Do not be afraid; God has heard the boy crying as he lies there. Lift the boy up and take him by the hand, for I will make him into a great nation.' Then God opened her eyes and she saw a well of water. So she went and filled the skin with water and gave the boy a drink" (Gen. 21:17-19).

I began to see this story through different eyes. What Hagar longed for is what we all long for – acceptance and a home. Yet she was a foreigner. She didn't really fit, even though she bore Abraham a son.

I think there are two main observations we can make from this story:

1. God Sends us Into Situations So We Can See Him at Work

It surprises me that God gave the OK for Abraham to kick out Hagar and Ishmael. "But God said to him [Abraham], "Do not be so distressed about the boy and your maidservant. Listen to whatever Sarah tells you ... because I will make the son of the maidservant into a nation also, because he is your offspring" (21:12-12, brackets mine).

But then again, this is God we're talking about. He always has a reason and purpose for everything. And His purpose for Hagar and Ishmael was for them to be sent away. The question is why?

Think about it: Why does God allow us to suffer or be rejected or disappointed? Why does God *send* us into difficult situations?

For Hagar, God wanted to get her attention. She had nothing but her son, a skin of water and some food which quickly ran out. She was desperate. She was alone. She was at the end of her rope.

All Hagar could do was weep. But God intervened and said, "Do not be afraid ... Lift the boy up and take him by the hand, for I will make him into a great nation" (21:17b-18). Amazing! In Hagar's darkest time, when she believed that she and Ishmael would die of dehydration, God revealed Himself *in* her hardship and gave her a promise.

This is why displacement is vital to our spiritual growth. For it is in our darkest times, when we feel isolated and alone and don't think we can go on another day, that God shows up. And He shows up by taking us out of ourselves and showing us His purpose. He gives us the reasons why we are in the situation we are in.

You see, God wanted Hagar to be sent away and rejected so He could reveal His plan to her: He would make her son the father of a great nation.

When I think about all the problems in the Middle East today and the challenges I face in trying to engage in my own community in Dearborn, I think of this story. God has a purpose for the Middle East. He is in control. He made that really clear to Hagar and Ishmael. And He makes it really clear today as I have met people from the Middle East who have been touched by God and have come to faith in Christ.

2: God Reveals His Purposes in Our Brokenness and Pain

God works in our brokenness and pain. This is, I believe, how God gets our attention and wakes us up to what He is doing.

As I've already mentioned, Jesus pushed His disciples to the very limit of their endurance in the upper room. And then at Gethsemane, everything unraveled. But that was God's purpose. Later, the disciples would remember the words of their Master and take His message of love to the world.

It was in Hagar's time of deepest despair that God showed up. "Then God opened her eyes and she saw a well of water. So she went and filled the skin with water and gave the boy a drink. God was with the boy as he grew up" (21:19-20).

Did the well magically appear to Hagar? No. She just hadn't seen it. When we are in pain and feel alone, our eyesight becomes very narrowly focused. We have a hard time seeing what is on the periphery – including what God is doing.

That is why it is vital when you feel discouraged or alone or in pain to turn to God. *God, what are you trying to show me in this? What am I not seeing?* And He will open your eyes to what He's doing.

This is why I believe *Pilgrim's Progress* is still one of the best-selling books of all time. Bunyan wrote it while he was in prison in England for refusing to stop preaching the gospel.

He couldn't stop doing what God had called him to do. And it cost him twelve years in prison away from his wife and four children. Instead of giving in to bitterness and despair, Bunyan turned to God. As a result, he wrote *Pilgrim's Progress,* and the world has never been the same since.

God reveals Himself in our brokenness and desperation. He uses us as tools for His purposes when we aren't relying on ourselves. It's at those times that we tend to see the larger purposes of God's plan. Our work, then, becomes meaningful because we're not trying to build up our ego or make a name for ourselves. It becomes all about Him. His glory. His Love. Changing the world.

So the next time you feel you are being pushed out in the desert, alone, unsure if you can take even one more step, open your eyes to the well right next to you. It is a well of living water. God Himself. He satisfies. He refreshes. He is the One who gives you purpose and meaning. May we see what Hagar saw – God's purposes amid the barrenness of life.

Reflections From The Alley

1. Can you relate to Hagar? If so, in what way?

2. How have you seen God at work in your pain and difficult circumstances?

Lord, may I learn from Hagar. In a lot of ways, I am just like her. Sometimes I feel unwanted and pushed aside. But instead of turning from You and focusing only on myself, help me to see You at work. Open my eyes to Your well. You are what I need. Align me to Your purposes, I pray. In Your name, Amen.

Chapter 17

TRAINING: Embracing God's Way of Maturity

"This cannot be a team of common men, because common men go nowhere. You have to be uncommon." (Herb Brooks)

There was nothing common about him. He was intense and spoke with passion. He played "Eye of the Tiger," the theme song from *Rocky*, in class. And he loved words. "Words are power," he'd often say. This uncommon man changed my life.

I'll never forget the first day I met him. It was the first semester of my junior year of college and I had registered for a communications class. Dr. Hensley was a new professor and quickly became the talk of the campus. The first day of class, he wrote his name on the board, turned to us and said, "I am not Mr. Rogers ... I don't like you the way you are. I want you to be better!" And he repeated it – a couple of times – until we got the point.

Most of us did not take him seriously. *Who is this guy?* I thought. *This class will be easy.* Boy, was I wrong. Dr. Hensley, a prolific writer of more than thirty books and many articles, was not easy; nor would he let any of his students produce second-best work.

"If you think you can slide by in this class and pass," he said, "you are wrong. I want you to give me your very best." On the first assignment I handed in – an essay, I believe – I got a D. There were red marks all over the paper. Dr. Hensley caught every spelling and grammatical mistake I made. It wasn't like my other classes; he expected perfection. He wrote a comment on my paper that went something like this: "Mr. Arnold, I expect better work from you. I know you can do better."

But I didn't do better. In fact, I did worse. A few weeks later, I got an F on a paper. His comment hit me right in the gut: "Mr. Arnold, you are currently the worst student in the class. Is this all I can expect from you? I believe you can do better if you really want to."

I was determined to show him what I was made of. I refused to be the worst student in the class. From that day forward, I took my assignments very serious and worked diligently on my writing and grammar.

There was steady improvement. My grades went up to Cs and then Bs, and then finally, an A. He wrote on my paper: "Mr. Arnold, you are the most improved student in the class. I am proud of you. I knew you could do it." Next to his comment he wrote the initials: E.O.T.T. – "Eye of the Tiger."

In my senior year I took a literature class by Dr. Hensley and it was by far my favorite class in college. But it wasn't the class or the reading that made it great. It was the professor. Dr. Hensley gave me a gift – the gift of loving words. When he read poetry or short stories he did so with such passion, evoking imagery and pathos.

A Much Needed Push

I owe this professor – more than anyone – for inspiring me to become a writer. What Dr. Hensley taught me, however, was much more than writing. He taught me the valuable lesson that we should always give our best and never give up.

The truth is, we all need people in our lives who push us, who inspire us on to new heights and encourage us to give our very best. In our fallen nature we tend to be lazy. We like shortcuts, the easy way out, and doing just enough to get by. But God wants us to give our very best.

We have one life to live, and *how* we live it matters greatly. We are called to live meaningfully and engage in meaningful work.

Jesus demonstrated this lesson to His disciples in the upper room. He pushed them so they would rely on His strength and words and carry out the meaningful work of His Kingdom. And He gave them this example: Serve and love others, just as He had served and loved them (see John 13). Indeed, He prepared them for the ultimate test of faith – His death and resurrection.

Jesus said to them, "Peace I leave with you; my peace I give you. I do not give to you as the world gives. Do not let your hearts be troubled and do not be afraid (John 14:27). Don't lose heart. Don't give up.

Don't give way to fear. Fear robs us of hope. Fear paralyzes us and shouts, *You can't. You won't.*

Fear is the result of us being out of control, which in turn is a result of the Fall. And I am convinced the way we overcome our fears and relinquish control is through being pushed to the limit.

Let me explain. I believe God places us in situations that force us to trust Him, allowing us to go through certain trials and difficulties which will lead us to turn away from our self-sufficient maneuvering to total dependency on Him. God wants us to live by hope – the hope that *only* He can rescue us, *only* He can sustain us, and *only* He can keep us going one more day.

Inspired to Hope

Hope changes a person. If we have no hope, what do we have, especially living in a world like ours? Dr. Martyn Lloyd-Jones said, "There are always two sides to the gospel; there is a pulling down and a raising up."[1] In the upper room, Jesus had to pull His disciples down so He could raise them up. He took away their false hopes, their delusions of power, their self-sufficiency – so He could lead them to become mature, confident, and hopeful in Him.

The late Herb Brooks, the coach of the 1980 USA Olympic Hockey team, knew what buttons to push to get his players to give their very best. He inspired them to hope and helped them believe the impossible could become possible.

The story of the *Miracle on Ice* is one of my favorites, a classic David-versus-Goliath tale. Brooks was one very unique and hard-headed coach. His coaching style was very intense and rigid. But he was the best college hockey coach in the country. His mission was to shake American hockey out of its slumber and beat the undefeated Soviet team.

Brooks was selected to coach the US Olympic team for the games being held in Lake Placid, New York. The team was comprised of college kids, mostly from the universities of Boston and Minnesota. They were by far the youngest team in the 1980 Olympics. Nobody

---

1 Lloyd-Jones, *Studies in the Sermon on the Mount,* 33.

thought the U.S. team would do well, especially against Russia. The Soviets dominated world hockey, having won the gold in the previous four Winter Olympics.

In the 2004 movie, Herb Brooks (played by Kurt Russell) states his case to the Olympic committee: "My plan is to adopt a new style. A hybrid of the Soviet School and Canadian School. A combination that requires the highest level: conditioning, speed, creativity, and most of all, team chemistry." The committee questioned his theories and told Brooks there was no way the U.S. could beat Russia.

"My goal is to beat them at their own game," Brooks told his team, referring to the Soviets. To do so, he pushed his players, working and conditioning them rigorously, constantly threatening to cut a player from the team if he slacked off. "If you give me 99%, you make my job very, very easy."[2]

Belief

Because of this training, the players worked together, made sacrifices, and developed amazing chemistry. Most importantly, they believed they *could* beat the best hockey team in the world. And because of their coach and the players' discipline and sacrifice, one of the greatest sports moments in American history occurred. The U.S. beat the Soviets in Lake Placid and then went on to beat Finland for the gold medal.

Right before Herb Brooks died (sadly, before the movie was released), I heard him say in an interview regarding his Olympic team: "A lot of these guys had never been pushed like that, never pulled. And I wasn't trying to put greatness into anybody; I was trying to pull it out. I don't like coaches that try to put in greatness because they think they've got all the answers. You've got to believe in them, have high standards of them, and pull it out."[3]

---

2 O'Connor, *Miracle on Ice*.

3 O'Connor, "Herb Brooks interview."

Greatness

I think this is what God does. He doesn't push us for no good reason. He pulls the greatness out of us, our God-given, image-bearing greatness. It's in there. But it's often smothered and pushed down by the world and by our own sinful nature. So God puts us in situations to pull out this greatness. He believes in us. He has called us. He knows fear will destroy us and He knows how hard it is to survive in this world, which is why He came.

When I pray and ask the Lord for help in a certain area – say, a certain area where I need to trust Him – He will always act on my prayer. That is to say He will put me into a certain situation or circumstance where I have to *work out* my prayer.

It's really easy to pray, "Lord, help me be patient" or "Help me be humble." But when the help comes (the situation, the difficult person, the temptation), it's at that time our faith either grows or withers.

Even as I write this, I have been praying about certain areas of my life where I need to surrender control and trust God. I pray every day in my morning prayers: "Lord, I give You control today." I pray 2 Corinthians 5:14 that the love of Christ would control me. Later on in my day, or sometime in the week, a situation will happen where I have to make the choice of trusting God or trying to take control.

This is what training is all about – choices. We make choices every day: choices to love or hate; choices to hope or despair; choices to engage in meaningful work or passivity. On it goes. We have to make the choice, but then God helps us to carry it out.

Nothing worthwhile and meaningful ever comes easily or without sacrifice.

Making Sacrifices for the Known

I think God is a lot like Dr. Hensley and Herb Brooks in pushing us to do better. Don't misunderstand. God absolutely loves you the way you are ... but He doesn't stop there. His desire is for you to become full-grown sons and daughters, mature, steadily trusting in Him, and not giving in to fear.

To accomplish this, He will push and mold and stretch you to your very limit. Think of it as training and conditioning. God is the ultimate coach. At times it may feel like He pushes too much, that He is a cruel coach. But He's not. He knows what you need and He knows how much to push.

We all need to be pushed in life. We respect those who do the pushing, and we are thankful how much they care about us. God loves us and cares about us so much that He allows difficult and uncertain situations to arise. He knows one of the best teachers in life is circumstances, especially challenging ones.

Think about the movies or books we like. The main character, the protagonist, must go through conflict and challenges or we'll lose interest and think he or she is a phony. That's what keeps us reading or watching – *How will he handle this? Will she love him even though he betrayed her? How will she get out of this mess?*

What we long to see on the big screen or in a novel is character transformation. If the character doesn't change – if he doesn't give up his executive job to save his marriage, or she doesn't track down her father and forgive him – we lose hope. And who wants that? There is enough hopelessness out there. No, we *want* hope. We long for it.

Herb Brooks would often say to his players, "You must make sacrifices for the unknown." He was trying to help them see beyond the here and now, and to hope for what *could* be.

As followers of Jesus we are called to make sacrifices for the *known*, for we know what God has promised and what awaits us. In the meantime, we are called to never lose sight of the truth that God believes in us and wants to transform us and make us all that He designed us to be.

Reflections From the Alley

1. Have you ever had a person in your life who really pushed you because they cared and wanted you to give your best? Who was the person? How did you handle it?

2. How have you seen God push you to grow and be the person He wants you to be?

Lord, thank You for pushing me. I know I need it. I need to face conflict and trials so I don't grow complacent or apathetic. Help me to see that You allow things to happen because You want me to transform and grow into the person You've created me to be. Help me not lose hope, but to constantly strive to grow more and bring You glory. In Jesus' name, Amen.

Chapter 18

RESTORATION: Learning to See God's Ultimate Plan

"Our ancestors came from Eden. We are headed toward a New Earth.
Meanwhile, we live out our lives on a sin-corrupted Earth, between
Eden and the New Earth, but we must never forget that this is not our
natural state." (Randy Alcorn)

A little over a year ago, I sat with my friend from Iraq as he tutored me in Arabic. It was the month of Ramadan, the ninth month of the Islamic calendar where Muslims fast from sunrise to sunset. They cannot eat or drink anything during the daylight hours. Instead they are instructed to use their time for reflection, repentance, humility, and submission to God.

Although my Iraqi friend would consider himself a nominal Muslim, he nevertheless observes Ramadan. I asked him, "What do you hope to get out of Ramadan?"

He paused for a moment and then said, "Well ... it is my hope that if I do good during Ramadan – good in fasting and praying– then God will overlook my faults later on." I asked him to explain more.

"For Muslims," he told me, "We hope that during this month God will overlook the bad things we do, especially if we do well during Ramadan."

"But what if you don't do well?" I asked. "What if you don't fast well or pray enough?"

"Well," he said, "I still hope God will forgive me."

Atonement

I thought about what my friend said. And you know what? I do the same thing at times. I can easily fall into the performance trap and think, *If I'm good enough or if I pray really hard and or go to church every Sunday, God will overlook my sins and I will be OK.* Granted, we don't take one month out of the year to fast and try to make up for all the sins we've committed. But I do think it's easy to slip into this mindset.

As my conversation with my Iraqi friend continued that day, I shared with him about the reason we need a Savior and atonement. I told him about the story of the Garden of Eden in Genesis. I told him every human being is trying to get back to the Garden. To be perfect. To walk with God and each other in perfect peace.

But we can't. Sin has made a mess of things. Our first parents blew it – a belief, by the way that Muslims adhere to as well, although they don't believe in original sin as the Bible teaches. My friend listened intently.

We are all in need of atonement, of God's covering of grace, mercy and love. Only Christ can cover us and make us whole. Other religions attempt to earn God's favor or make a way up to God. But that's impossible. Thankfully, instead He came down to us.

When the first offense and rebellion occurred, God gave a promise to one day make all things right again, to make us right again, so that once again we can live as God intended (see Genesis 3:15-21).

In a sense, then, the life of faith is not only a progression toward God, but also a returning back to what we had in Eden.

Drugged By Grief

The mood changes dramatically as Jesus guides His disciples out of the city and down into the valley to one of His favorite spots – an olive garden called Gethsemane. John records that this spot is where Jesus and His disciples met often (John. 18:2). As a result, Judas the betrayer knew exactly where to lead the authorities to arrest Jesus.

En route to the garden Jesus spoke with the disciples about the importance of remaining (or abiding) with Him, just as a branch remains with the vine (John 15). "I've told you these things to prepare you for rough times ahead," Jesus tells them (John 16:1).[1]

Jesus could see the grief in His disciples' eyes. He could see their dreams, their hopes for a better life, for their nation, for the Jewish

1 The Message.

people who had for so long endured Roman oppression, rapidly slipping away each step they took toward the olive garden.

The night air was cool. The sounds of the Passover celebration ceased. The city walls loomed in the distance, hushed by the darkness of night. The darkness thickened the farther they moved away from the city and entered the garden.

As Jesus went off to pray for the strength to face what was about to come, His disciples were fast asleep. *The Message* version says, "He got up from prayer, went back to the disciples and found them asleep, drugged by grief" (Luke 22:46).[2]

Drugged by grief. What powerful imagery. When I am at my lowest, when I feel the most alone and depressed, I just want to get into bed, bury my head in the pillow, and sleep. It's a way to escape grieving, at least for a while. When we are depressed and the world feels cold and dark, we don't want to get out of bed. Perhaps we hope the darkness will lift if we stay under the covers a little longer. I believe this is what the disciples were experiencing.

The disciples were shell-shocked. They had expected to celebrate a very normal, traditional Passover meal. But it was not to be. Feeling confused, distraught, and depressed, all they longed to do was sleep. Three times, in fact, Jesus had to come and rouse them from their slumber. But all they craved was to escape their sorrow in sleep. When the betrayer, Judas, came with a band of soldiers, the disciples' grief turned to panic and they fled.

Broken Dreams

Peter completely disassociated himself from Jesus, denying him three times, just as Jesus said he would. For a Jewish disciple to deny his Rabbi was unthinkable – it meant he had forever severed their relationship. No wonder Peter wept and then reverted to his old, familiar job of fishing. His grief drugged him into complete hopelessness and back to his life before he met Jesus.

So deep was the disciples' grief and so broken were their dreams, that even after the women reported that the tomb was empty and an

---

2 The Message.

angel had appeared to them announcing Jesus had risen, they still didn't believe He was alive.

What do we do when we are drugged by grief? How do we get up from the slumber of broken dreams? The answer, I believe, lies in the word *restoration.*

The story of restoration came dramatically into effect shortly after Jesus was raised from the grave.

One of Satan's major strategies in this world is to get followers of Jesus to feel so ashamed of how badly they failed Him that they're convinced Christ has disowned them. So they give up and go back to their old way of life. Satan wants nothing more than for us to give up on our dreams, to give up on ourselves, an ultimately, to give up on God.

For some, this means returning to a life of mediocrity, settling for a job or a calling that is second-best, and not fulfilling or meaningful. For others it is return to an addiction like alcohol or food. Satan will do everything he can to get you to think God has given up on you. That you don't belong anymore. That God will never take you back.

So Peter went up north, back to Galilee, to try his hand in fishing again. Unfortunately for him, it wasn't working out too well. I can just imagine him thinking: *I'm a failure as a disciple; now, I can't even fish. I really messed up! God must be really mad.*

But then something unexpected happened. Peter and the others noticed someone on the shore. But they didn't recognize it was Jesus (John 21:4). Jesus said, "Hey, did you catch any fish for breakfast?" Peter and the others were probably a bit miffed at this question. "Throw your net on the right side of the boat and you will find some," Jesus continued (John 21:6). When they did, there were so many fish that they couldn't even pull the net up into the boat.

Reinstatement

It was at that moment Peter realized who was on the beach. It's interesting what happened next. Jesus told Peter to bring some fish so He could cook breakfast. He didn't scold Peter. He didn't ask, "What are you doing back fishing?" He didn't bring up the past. He served him and loved him – and made breakfast.

When Satan tries to convince us that God would never take us back or would never forgive that certain sin, it's a flat-out lie. God picks us back up again, serves us, and loves us. After breakfast, Jesus says to Peter, "Do you love me?" (John 21:15-17). He says it three times in fact. "Do you love me more than these fish?" He then tells Peter to feed and shepherd His sheep.

This is called reinstatement.

To reinstate someone means to restore that person back to a previous position or condition. This is what Jesus did with Peter. He restored his dream and calling. He said, "You belong to Me. Nobody can take that away from you."

What God Does

Randy Alcorn says, "Reconcile. Redeem. Restore. Recover. Return. Renew. Regenerate. Resurrect. Each of these biblical words begins with the re-prefix, suggesting a return to an original condition that was ruined or lost."[3]

This is what God does – He restores. He restores us, and one day, He will restore the world which He created. He is the Great Restorer.

"God always sees us in the light of what he intended us to be, and he always seeks to *restore* us to that design."[4] This is the hope we need to keep going, especially in those times when the enemy tries to deceive us into thinking our sins condemn us and there's no release. Only God can restore us and restore our dreams. We cannot. And we cannot work our way back to Him, thinking, "If only I do better in prayer, better in reading the Bible, better in loving my spouse, *then* ..."

No. All we have to do is *allow* God to have all of us. We cannot reinstate ourselves. We can't work hard enough to earn His favor. All we can do is give ourselves to Him and long for the restoration we will experience one day. Indeed, even now there will be partial restoration – Peter is an example of that.

---

3 Alcorn, *Heaven,* 88.

4 Ibid., 88.

But one day there will be *ultimate restoration*. All our dreams will come true. We will finally be all that God has created us to be.

Reflections From the Alley

1. Have you ever been "drugged by grief"? What got you through it?

2. How have you seen God restore?   How is God the Great Restorer?

Lord, You are the Great Restorer. You are the One who reinstates me, who helps me dream again and hope again. I thank You for the atonement, for covering me with Your mercy and grace. Help me to hold on to the hope that You are restoring all things, including me. I give You my life today; use it as You'd like. In Jesus' name, Amen.

Chapter 19

CONSUMMATION: The End of Displacement

"Furthermore, while the kingdom has been inaugurated in the incarnation, death, and resurrection of Jesus (it is full, complete, and irreversible), it is not yet fully consummated, and so we live in an in-between time, a time after its inauguration and before its completion in the return of Christ." (Michael Frost and Alan Hirsch)

What amazes me the most about the Jewish Holocaust survivors is not only were they able to reestablish their lives – get married, have children, celebrate the Jewish holy days – but they also wrote and learned and created. They published newspapers; they reengaged the arts.

They applied their gifts and talents to something good and beautiful. They breathed new life into dreams that they once feared were dead and buried forever.

They rediscovered hope.

But it wasn't easy. Hope never is. Sometimes it takes a while for hope to push through the hard, cold soil of disillusionment and pain. One day, however, after the sun comes out and the rain comes down and the ground softens, hope sprouts up, releasing a fragrance of life and meaning and achievement.

For the Jewish Holocaust survivors, hope pushed up through the horrors of war and death and displacement in the form of meaningful work. And that was a big deal. Why?

Holes

One of the many cruel ways the Nazis attempted to break the will of the Jews and strip away their hope was by forcing them to dig holes for hours and hours and then refill them. It was meaningless labor, intended to completely humiliate and devalue them.

Similarly, when you are unsure of God's purpose for your life and find yourself just existing – going through the motions of life – it's like digging hole after hole and then filling them back up. It's a waste. It's unproductive.

When we are displaced and disillusioned in this life, it's easy to be discouraged and lose sight of the bigger picture. We find ourselves beaten down by life, just as the Jews were beaten down by the Nazis. And we get stuck in a hole, unsure of how to get out or even what to do after – or if – we do get out.

This was the case for God's people about three thousand years ago. The Israelites found themselves in a gigantic hole, uncertain of how to get out. But God had something to teach them.

The Letter

God spoke to His people through a love letter. You see, after years and years of turning from God, losing their passion and purpose, God said enough's enough. So He allowed the largest and most dominant empire in the world at that time – the Babylonians – to come in, destroy Jerusalem, and exile the survivors to live and labor in Babylon. Talk about a deep, dark hole!

This is what God said in His letter, recorded by His prophet, Jeremiah:

"This is what the LORD Almighty, the God of Israel, says to all those I carried into exile from Jerusalem to Babylon: 'Build houses and settle down; plant gardens and eat what they produce. Marry and have sons and daughters; find wives for your sons and give your daughters in marriage, so that they too may have sons and daughters. Increase in number there; do not decrease. Also, seek the peace and prosperity of the city to which I have carried you into exile. Pray to the LORD for it, because if it prospers, you too will prosper.' Yes, this is what the LORD Almighty, the God of Israel, says: 'Do not let the prophets and diviners among you deceive you. Do not listen to the dreams you encourage them to have. They are prophesying lies to you in my name. I have not sent them,' declares the LORD. This is what the LORD says: 'When seventy years are completed for Babylon, I will come to you and fulfill my good promise to bring you back to this place. For I know the plans I have for you,' declares the LORD, 'plans to prosper you and not to harm you, plans to give you hope and a future. Then you will call on me and come and pray to me, and I will listen to you. You will seek me and find me when you seek me with all your heart. I will be found by you,' declares the LORD, 'and will bring you back from captivity. I will gather you from all the nations and places where I have banished you,' declares the LORD, 'and will bring you back to the place from which I carried you into exile.'" (Jeremiah 29:4-14).

New Home

This letter was much-needed because false prophets had told the exiles lies about their current situation. They foolishly told them their stay in Babylon was only temporary, and that everything would soon get back to normal.

God's letter, however, said basically the opposite: "Sorry, you'll be here for seventy years. So get on with it. Live meaningful lives. Bless people and reach out to those who don't know Me. Don't be bitter. Don't listen to phony promises of a normal life back home. This is your new home."

It was a hard pill to swallow. But God was serious. He knew this would be a time of great testing and stretching for His people.

The good news was some listened and learned to thrive in displacement. The prophet Daniel, for example, did what God told them to do. He and a few of his friends lived out the Kingdom of God in the midst of a wicked and pagan empire (See Daniel 1).

We are called to do the same. God's letter to the exiles was filled with deep compassion and purpose and love. God didn't want His people digging holes and refilling them, wasting their time and growing hopeless. He had a plan. A master plan. He told them there will come a day when displacement will end and He would take them home. One day there will be consummation.

God's Purpose

The idea of consummation is bringing something to completion or fruition; it is the act of making something whole or one. "For this reason a man shall leave his father and his mother, and be joined to his wife; and they shall become one flesh" (Genesis 2:24).[1] This is consummation.

And this is what will happen one day when we are joined with the Bridegroom, Christ, who will make us one with Himself. Paul says that God's purpose is to "bring all things in heaven and on earth together under one head, even Christ" (Eph. 1:10).

> "We are exiles. But we're exiles called to a great purpose. Called out of digging holes to moving mountains."

We long for this consummation. We believe it will happen, but we are like ships lost at sea. We cannot find the harbor, our final destination, and safety. And so we live our lives adrift in a culture that wants nothing to do with godliness. We are exiles. But we're exiles called to a great purpose. God has called us to stop digging holes and start moving mountains.

So how do we live and move toward this consummation? I think there are a couple of principles we must consider, all of which, I believe, can be drawn from the story of God's people living as exiles in Babylon.

Do you remember the three stages or aspects we looked at in the introduction to this section? They are: sentness, meaningful work, and longing.

1. Sentness

To be sent is all about movement, the willingness to go and the knowledge that this going is purposeful and meaningful. God's people are a sent people. It was, after all, God who sent His people into displacement: "This is what the LORD Almighty, the God of Israel,

---

1 NASB.

says to all those I carried into exile from Jerusalem to Babylon" (Jer. 29:4).

Here's the truth about sentness:

God sends us into different environments and places to **(1) stretch our faith** so we will trust in Him, and **(2) to use us for His purposes** to impact others. Think about it.

- God called Moses out of Egypt where he was pruned and trained in the desert, and then back to Egypt to deliver his enslaved countrymen (Exodus 3-4).
- Gideon was literally hiding out in a winepress (a hole in the ground) when God called him to lead an army (Judges 6).
- In the beginning of the book of Acts, the gospel movement was predominately in a Jewish context until some unknown Jewish believers from Cyprus and Cyrene decided to step out in faith and take the message to the Greeks in Antioch (Acts 11:19-30).

This is a common thread throughout the Bible: God calls His people into foreign environments to pull off great feats that can only be achieved by God working powerfully through His people. Through us!

2. Meaningful Work

God called His people who were living in exile in Babylon to get on with life – to marry, have children, build houses, get jobs. He told them specifically to increase in number. He called them to live and work meaningfully.

Instead of resisting or rebelling against their new masters, He called them to prosper: "Seek the peace and prosperity of the city to which I have carried you into exile. Pray to the LORD for it, because if it prospers, you too will prosper" (Jeremiah 29:7).

When you hear the word "prosper," you may be tempted to think of material gain. The Hebrew word for "prosper," however, is *shalom*. This is a rich word, depicting the idea of living out every aspect of life in wholeness and fullness. It is holistic.

Shalom should touch every area of our lives: our relationships, our vocations, how we communicate, how we spend our money. It goes beyond mere happiness and emotional highs. It's the attitude of our hearts, of something deep within, a sense we are doing what we're meant to do and living the way we're meant to live.

Shalom is how God calls us to live – experiencing His best, living out His fullness in every aspect of life.

Henry Conn and Manuel Ortiz wrote, "To seek the peace and good of the city meant to spend one's energies and activity in praying for its peace and blessing by the doing of good works. Urban refugees were to be urban public benefactors."[2]

The exiles, in other words, were positioned to be a blessing in one of the most secular yet influential cities in the world. Remember, these exiles were forced out of their homes and city and taken captive to a new city and culture. This meant they had to learn a new language, were exposed to new ideologies and religions, and yet were called by God to be good neighbors to the very enemy who had destroyed their city, their hopes, and their dreams.

Is it any wonder, then, there were so-called prophets who were telling the exiles to dissociate themselves from evil Babylon and that their time away from Jerusalem would only be temporary?

But that is not what God said. The letter Jeremiah delivered was most likely a big shock to the exiles. *What? God wants us to move into the city of Babylon, build houses, marry and have children? This sounds like slavery in Egypt all over again!*

Is it any different than the disciples' shock in the upper room at Passover? Or the shock Moses faced when God spoke to him from a bush and called him to go back to Egypt and free His people from slavery? But this is how God works. It's never predictable. It defies human logic. It most certainly isn't comfortable or safe.

And the reason God does this is so we will live meaningful lives, carrying out work that is life-giving and of eternal value.

Don't misunderstand. I'm not talking about a pain-free life where everything goes our way. I'm saying God wants us to live life intentionally. For some, like my friend Carl, it's taking a huge risk and starting a new business. For others, like Fiko, it's sacrificing a big

---

2 Conn and Ortiz, *Urban Ministry*, 102.

salary for a rewarding job serving vulnerable refugees. For my wife, meaningful work is staying home taking care of our two-year-old.

Here's the truth about meaningful work:

God sends us into difficult environments and circumstances to **(1) use us** to do extraordinary things for His Kingdom, and **(2) get us to see** people through His eyes so that we can love them with His love.

The Jewish people had forgotten the God of Moses, the One who split the Red Sea. They became comfortable and lazy, living in a divided land.

God wanted His people to no longer rely on their rituals and their Temple, and because they were His chosen people, they could do what they wanted and He would always look after them.

Did God expect them to fit in? No. Were they to lose their identity? Absolutely not. Just the opposite. They were to thrive in their God-given, God-anointed identity as His people in a dark and pagan land – to show the Babylonians the love of God and that they too will flourish when they give their lives to Him.

God wanted Babylon to know His *shalom*. And He wants our world – our communities, our jobs, our schools, our families – to know His *shalom*. This is His purpose: To use us to spread His love throughout the world.

We are His exiles living in a modern-day Babylon. But we won't be here forever. God's purpose doesn't end here. There's more. There will be a final consummation.

Longing

The reason that God's people could live such prosperous lives in a pagan city was because of the promise God gave them: "'When seventy years are completed for Babylon, I will come to you and fulfill my good promise to bring you back to this place. For I know the plans I have for you,' declares the LORD, 'plans to prosper you and not to harm you, plans to give you hope and a future'" (Jeremiah 29:10-11).

These verses reveal why God's love letter to His people, whom He had displaced and sent into exile, is so incredible. God reminded them that *He* is in control. *He* has a purpose for them. *He* hasn't forgotten them. Nor is He indifferent to their hopes, longings and dreams.

If God were to write you a love letter, I believe He would speak a similar message: *I have a purpose for you in your modern-day Babylon. I want you to see My glory. I want all the nations to know that I am the Lord – and it's through you I will deliver this message. But there will be a day where I will bring you back to your true home. I will restore you. All your dreams will come true and all your longings will be met. There will be consummation. But not yet ... I have a lot of work to do before that.*

Biblical scholar Charles Fienberg wrote: "The Lord assures [the exiles] that despite their surmise as to his lack of concern for their plight, he had not forgotten them. Regardless of appearances to the contrary, the Lord was not denying them hope for the future; it would not be realized immediately or in the near future ... This word from the Lord was surely more heartening to the exiles' spirits than the false prophets' promises of quick deliverance."[3]

The key concept for those in exile, then as now, lies in the word "seek." As pilgrims and sojourners, we are called to seek God for our deliverance, His ultimate plan to bring us to Himself. This is what makes Jeremiah 29:11 so powerful. As displaced persons, God invites us to call out to Him, to seek Him with every part of our being. "You will seek me and find me *when you seek me* with all your heart" (29:13, italics mine).

This is why our longing for a better world, for what Jesus promised when He said He would go to prepare a place for us, must not be lost in the everyday circumstances of life. God wants to take our longing for deliverance and fulfillment and use it to change the world.

Think of Daniel. He was an exile. Because of his amazing ability to interpret dreams combined with a steadfast faith in the God of Israel, he rose to a powerful position in Babylon. Daniel didn't forget his identity as a child of God, even though secularism and great trials were all around him. God blessed Daniel because his hope was not in the seen world he lived in; it was in the world to come.

I've often wondered, months after that climactic and sorrowful night in the upper room, if the disciples looked back to that night as the event that forged them together for the purpose of reaching the world

---

3 Fienberg, "Jeremiah," 555.

with the gospel. After all, each gospel writer – Matthew, Mark, Luke and John – recorded the events of the Last Supper. John went into the most detail, devoting five chapters (13-17) to it.

I look back on the most painful and trying times of my life – the tumor in my right leg that required intensive surgery, being betrayed by people who had been close to me, facing near burnout and exhaustion from work – as being the most profitable to my faith. For it was in those times that I sensed God's presence in a strong way, even though at the time I didn't understand why I was going through these trials.

Why? Because in that moment, I was desperate for God. I knew I couldn't get through it without Him. It caused me to turn my eyes away from myself and from the world, and to long for God and His peace with more intensity.

One of the greatest lessons I have learned from working with refugees and immigrants is their hopeful perspective on life. For most of them, there is a longing to return to their country of origin. Many, unfortunately, may never have that chance. But that hope and desire lies within them.

So it is with us – we continue to hope and seek after God until finally, *finally* consummation will take place and we will be with Him forever.

This is God's plan, the Apostle Paul tells us. "To unify all things and head them up and consummate them in Christ, both things in heaven and things on earth" (Ephesians 1:10).[4] This is God's agenda, His purpose. We are part of His purpose ... the biggest part!

So I conclude with a challenge and a blessing. One day all will be made right. You will be made right. Consummation will take place.

In the meantime, learn to trust God with every ounce of your being and learn to love and give and serve others. If you do, I bet there will be a line of people waiting to talk with you in heaven who will say, "Thank you. Thank you for touching my life. Thank you for the words you spoke to me and how you loved me. Thank you for never giving up even when the world crashed down all around you."

May that be our aim as we learn to live out our faith in a world where we are utterly displaced.

---

4 Amplified Version.

Reflections From the Alley

1. Read again the passage in Jeremiah 29:4-14. What stands out to you? How does this apply to your life now?

2. Consider the three concepts mentioned in this chapter, sentness, meaningful work, longing. How can you see yourself as having been sent in your current situation? How does God want you to engage in meaningful work? How does living like this help you seek Christ and long for what awaits you in Heaven?

3. Write out a prayer here based on your answers to question. Ask God to shape you and mold you to do great things for Him.

EPILOGUE

Pilgrim Stories

The man with the pipe and the lady disappeared that day, quickly maneuvering through Chicago's endless alleys. But their memory has stayed with me. To this day, when I happen to drive or walk through an alley, I think of them.

The gift they gave me was their pursuit. They were so focused on finding something. And this, I believe, is how we need to live – in deep pursuit of God.

All of us are on a journey, a journey full of bends and twists, of sunny days and rainy days. The point is to keep going, to move steadily toward Christ and toward our ultimate destination. This is our pursuit.

Jesus told us He had to leave to prepare a place for us, and He promised He wouldn't leave us here in the alleys, alone and orphaned.

It's hard to wait. Life is not easy. Jesus warned us it wouldn't be. We are displaced people living in a land that is not our own. True, there are times when everything seems to be in harmony, when our soul sings and drinks deeply of life. But those times don't last ... at least not yet.

To conclude this book, I have attempted to capture the stories of two pilgrims, both of whom came as refugees to the United States and have amazing stories of courage, hope, and adventure. One is from Burma (Myanmar), and the other is from Iraq. Listen to their stories, soak them up, and be reminded that we are all exiles and refugees trying to find our way.

Thoo Lay: A Woman of Prayer

Thoo Lay lived a simple life raising her four children in a small village in the Karen State of Burma, located on the eastern border of Thailand. In 2002, however, her simple life came to a screeching halt. Burmese soldiers marched into her village and demanded that Thoo Lay's husband work for the military.

He refused due to the oppression and injustice of Myanmar's military, which has dominated the government for years, thus putting himself and his family in grave danger. At his refusal, the soldiers demanded he give them money. He told the soldiers he didn't have any money to give to them presently, but that he would sell some of his animals and give them the profit.

The offer did not satisfy the soldiers. They then proceeded to break into their home, searching frantically for money and, sadly, beat Thoo Lay's sister, who was living with the family. After the soldiers left, Thoo Lay and her husband had to make a decision. Their daughters were all in their early twenties and late-teens, and her son was newly-married. What would they do?

Thoo Lay did what she always had – she got on her knees and prayed, asking God to show her what to do. As she prayed, Thoo Lay had a peace from the Lord, knowing that God wanted them to flee their home. For if the soldiers came back, the outcome could be much worse.

So the family left everything: their home, their friends, and the majority of their belongings. "When the soldiers left," Thoo Lay said, "I didn't know what was next, what the future held. I didn't even pack our belongings, because we didn't want the soldiers to know we were leaving."

Another dilemma they faced was the rain. It was the rainy season in Burma, making it very difficult to travel up hills and through the jungle, where Thoo Lay and her family lived. "The day we fled I prayed and prayed that the rain would stop ... and it did! God answered my prayer and we were able to climb up the hills."

At midnight, Thoo Lay, her husband, their three daughters, and her son and daughter-in-law, headed out into the darkness of the jungle.

"At night," she continued, "it was so dark that we would hold each other's hands, unable to see anything in front of us." Sometimes the family would travel in the daylight, getting clues from their countrymen. (Burmese-Karen workers who worked in the jungles often worked undercover, telling the people when it was safe to move freely and that no Burmese soldiers had been spotted.)

Those clues helped, as well as teaming up with other Karen people in similar predicaments who were migrating eastward toward the Thai boarder.

"We traveled for a whole month. Thankfully, we only heard gunshots. We were never shot at. It was God's protection." I learned from Thoo Lay that if a Burmese soldier spotted a Karen person (or family) trying to escape to Thailand, they would shoot to kill. They were seen as insurgents, unwilling to submit to the Burmese government.

Through much prayer and sticking together, Thoo Lay and her family finally made it to the border of Thailand. Once they got there, they followed the masses of Karen people to one of Thailand's many refugee camps for displaced people.

For a majority of Karen people (including Thoo Lay and family), the camp they settled in was the Mae La camp in northwest Thailand, the largest Burmese refugee camp in Thailand. About ninety per cent of the refugees in that camp are the Karen people of Burma.

Finally, after a month of extreme danger, very little food and no sleep, Thoo Lay and her family were safe in this temporary shelter, in this city of refuge.

"We lived in the camp for six years," Thoo Lay said. "It was a blessing because everyone helped each other. Many gave us bags of rice and clothes. Everyone shared what they had. I am so grateful to God. He protected us all the way to Chicago."

After six years of living in the Mae La camp, Thoo Lay and her family were resettled to the United States. Thoo Lay, her husband, and one of her daughters were sent to Utica, New York. Her other two daughters, son, daughter-in-law and their two children, were sent to Chicago.

In 2007, I had the privilege of helping Thoo Lay's family find an apartment on Chicago's northwest side, as well as other essential adjustment services.

A year later, Thoo Lay and her husband moved from New York to join their family in Chicago. In 2008, my friend and I helped start a house church for the Burmese refugees in our neighborhood. Thoo Lay and her family joined the church and would often host our meetings. Thoo Lay was affectionately called, "Momma Moo," named so because of her daughter's first name.

Thoo Lay is as much of a prayer warrior as ever. She has a huge heart to see Burmese Buddhists come to faith in Christ, and a passion to awaken some of her own people (the Karen Christians) from their religious slumber. Although her English is limited, her heart for God is huge. She is, in my opinion, one of the blessed ones who Jesus talked about in Matthew 5. She has seen so much and has suffered so much. But her smile and joy are evident of her rock-solid faith in Jesus. She is a true pilgrim of the alley, whose treasures will overflow in heaven.

Yousif: Expressing God's Grace from the Middle East

The Apostle Paul says we are God's "workmanship, created in Christ Jesus to do good works, which God prepared in advance for us to do" (Ephesians 2:10). The idea behind the word "workmanship" is something created, such as a poem. Literally, we are God's poems, His expression, with His love and grace written on our hearts. [The Greek word is *poema*.] For my friend, Yousif, this is exactly how he understands God's plan for his life.

Yousif grew up in Baghdad, Iraq. At an early age, he was introduced to the fine arts. "I spent all my life with the arts," he said, "painting, music, sculpting, and theater. I went to Baghdad's fine arts college located in the center of the city." It was through his studies that Yousif was introduced to some of the masters in the art world. "I was inspired by Picasso, Rembrandt, and Raphael. When I studied them and other great artists, I learned about Christianity and about Jesus."

God used art to draw Yousif to Himself. "Even though I didn't understand anything about Christianity, most of my art work was about Jesus. I was drawn to Jesus. I made many crosses, some of which are still back in my home in Baghdad."

Yousif grew up in the Sabean-Mandean religion, a Gnostic-based religion that developed in the Middle East. Sabeans claim to be followers of John the Baptist, who, they say, is the final prophet. They believe in God, but reject Jesus as the Son of God and the Messiah.

"I was not very serious in this religion," Yousif commented. "Most Sabeans aren't. It's more of a tradition with a lot of myths. It's very confusing." Their main teaching, I learned from Yousif, centers on the act of baptism, which Sabeans believe is of primary importance. For them, baptism purifies both body and soul. As a result, a baby is baptized thirty days after birth, and adults can get baptized as many times as they want throughout their life.

"I left Iraq and moved to Jordan because life was too hard in Iraq," Yousif continued. "Especially for an artist, there was not much opportunity for me because of all the problems in Iraq."

And it was in Amman, Jordan, where Yousif felt the freedom to pursue his growing desire to learn about Jesus and the Bible which he had read in his art books. "When I first came to Amman, I happened to visit an Evangelical Free church. I went two times and then I accepted Jesus as my Savior with an Iraqi pastor."

Yousif's life was radically changed. What he had read about in his books at the university, specifically the Christ-focused art work from the Renaissance Period, now became a reality. Yousif realized God was wooing him his whole life.

Shortly after his conversion, Yousif wanted to use his talents for the Lord. "I began to love the church songs very much," he said. "I started to learn how to play guitar and eventually became the worship leader at the church."

Yousif also taught art classes to other students and young people, which enabled him to share his faith in Christ through art. "I also enrolled in the local seminary in Amman, taking Bible and theology classes," Yousif said. But in spite of his newfound faith and his involvement in ministry, Yousif felt a growing dissatisfaction living in the Middle East, especially as a refugee living in Jordan. So he applied for refugee status through the United Nations and was accepted to go to America. Yousif believed this was God's plan for him.

"It was my dream to come to America," Yousif told me. "I spent nine years in Jordan, which was great because I met Jesus. But something was missing."

I met Yousif a few years back when he first arrived in America as a refugee, where he was resettled to Chicago. We hit it off and I soon learned his story. Yousif started attending the church I pastored and became an active part of our faith community in the Lakeview neighborhood of Chicago.

After six months or so of his involvement with our church, Yousif moved to the Detroit-area where he knew more Iraqis. He also had a cousin living there. When my family and I moved to Detroit, Yousif and I reconnected.

Recently, Yousif told me, "America is difficult. I feel alone. I am single and sometimes feel isolated. But my hope is that God will use me to bring people – especially Muslim background people – to Jesus. I want to use my art to witness and motivate people toward Christ. I have many dreams and many projects I'd like to do."

God has a plan for Yousif. For it was God who created him to do good works for His Kingdom. Although it's hard for him living here as a foreigner in the midst of a recession, Yousif has not given up on his dream. I believe God has great things for Yousif to do ... and He's placed him right into the heart of the Muslim world in America – Detroit.

I know that you have dreams, too. You are God's poem. His masterpiece. A written example to express His love and grace to a world that desperately needs Him.

So with that I say thank you. Thank you for reading this book and for being on this journey with me. I hope to meet you someday. But if we don't meet in this world, we shall in the next!

I hope you find all the love and hope and joy that Christ wants to give to you while you wait for Him to come back and take you where He is.

Bibliography

Alcorn, Randy. *Heaven*. Tyndale: Wheaton, 2004.

Bly, Robert. *Iron John: A Book About Men*. Reading: Addison-Wesley, 1990.

Case, Steve. *God is Here: Connecting with Him in Everyday Life*. Orlando: Relevant, 2005.

Chambers, Oswald. *My Utmost For His Highest*. Grand Rapids: Discovery House, 1992.

Chesterton, G.K. *Orthodoxy*. New York: Image, 1908.

_____. *Napoleon of Notting Hill*. New York: Dover, 1991.

Claiborne, Shane, and Chris Haw. *Jesus for President: Politics for Ordinary Radicals*. Grand Rapids: Zondervan, 2008.

Clemetson, Lynette. "Bosnian's in America: A Two-Sided Saga." *The New York Times*, April 29, 2007. No pages. Online: http://www.nytimes.com/2007/04/29/us/29youth.html?pagewanted=all.

Conn, Harvie, and Manuel Ortiz. *Urban Ministry: The Kingdom, the City & The People*. Downers Grove: InterVarsity: 2001.

Cowman, L.B. *Streams in the Desert*. Grand Rapids: Zondervan, 1997.

Crabb, Larry. *Inside Out*. Colorado Springs: Navpress, 1988).

Duncan, Ligon. "Cities of Refuges." *The Gospel Coalition*. No pages. Online: http://www.thegospelcoalition.org/resources/search/a/numbers%2035.

Edmondstone, Michael. "History of Blues Music." April 18, 2008. No pages. Online: http://folkmusic.suite101.com/article.cfm/history_of_blues_music.

Eldredge, John. *Wild at Heart: Discovering the Secret of a Man's Soul*. Nashville: Nelson, 2001.

Fienberg, Charles. "Jeremiah" In *The Expositor's Bible Commentary*. Grand Rapids: Zondervan, 1986.

Frost, Michael, and Alan Hirsch. *The Shaping of Things to Come: Innovation and Mission for the 21st Century Church*. Peabody: Hendrickson, 2003.

_____. *The Faith of Leap: Embracing a Theology of Risk, Adventure & Courage*. Grand Rapids: Baker, 2011.

Gower, Ralph. *The Essential Bible: Manners and Customs*. Chicago: Moody, 2000.

Hellerman, Joseph. *When the Church Was a Family: Recapturing Jesus' Vision for Authentic Christian Community*. Nashville: Broadman and Holman, 2009.

Jackson, Peter. *The Lord of the Rings: Return of the King*. New Line Cinema, 2003.

Lawrence, Brother. *The Practice of the Presence of God with Spiritual Maxims*. Grand Rapids: Revell, 1967

L'Engle, Madeleine. *Walking on Water: Reflections on Faith and Art*. Colorado Springs: Shaw, 2001.

Lewis, C.S. *George MacDonald*. New York: HarperCollins, 1946.

_____. *The Weight of Glory*. San Francisco: Harper, 1949.

Lloyd-Jones, D. Martyn. *Studies in the Sermon on the Mount*. Grand Rapids: Eerdmans, 1959-60.

McManus, Erwin Raphael. *An Unstoppable Force: Daring to Become the Church God Had in Mind*. Colorado Springs: Group, 2001.

Merriam-Webster. "Wisdom." *Merriam-Webster's Online Dictionary*. No pages. Online: http://www.merriam-webster.com/dictionary/wisdom.

Nee, Watchman. *The Normal Christian Life*. Gospel Literature Service: Bombay, 1957.

O'Connor, Gavin. *Miracle*. Walt Disney Pictures, 2004.

Peterson, Eugene H. *The Contemplative Pastor: Returning to the Art of Spiritual Direction*. Grand Rapids: Eerdmans, 1989.

Public Broadcasting Service. "The Roman Empire in the First Century: Family Life." No pages. Online: www.pbs.org/empires/romans/empire/family.html.

Sailhamer, John H. *NIV Compact Bible Commentary*. Grand Rapids: Zondervan, 1994.

Schaeffer, Francis. *Trilogy: The God Who is There, Escape From Reason, and He is There and He is Not Silent*. Wheaton: Crossway, 1990.

United State Holocaust Memorial Museum. "Displaced Persons," *Holocaust Encyclopedia*. No pages. Online: http://www.ushmm.org/wlc/en/article.php?ModuleId=10005462.

Webber, Robert E. *Ancient Future Evangelism: Making Your Church a Faith-Forming Community*. Grand Rapids: Baker, 2003.

Yancey, Philip. *The Jesus I Never Knew*. Grand Rapids: Zondervan, 1995.

About the Author

Dave Arnold grew up in the D.C. Area. At the age of seventeen, he turned his life over to Christ through the ministry of Young Life. While in college at Taylor University-Fort Wayne, Dave received his calling into ministry. Since then, he has worked in a variety of roles: youth and college ministry, church planting, inner city missions, church planting consulting, and as a case manager with World Relief. Dave and his wife, Angie, have travelled all over the world working with the displaced, poor, and hurting. Dave has also been a freelance writer for the last ten years and a blogger for the last two years. He currently lives in the Dearborn (Detroit-area) where he works with immigrants from the Middle East. He is passionate about hospitality and helping "strangers" feel like they belong. Dave is married to Angie and they have one son, Luke.

You can connect with Dave online at www.reflectionsfromthealley.org or follow him on Twitter @davejarnold16.

Acknowledgements

Blaise Pascal once said that we should never say "my book," but rather, "our book, because in general they contain much more of what belongs to other people than to themselves."

This is certainly true for me and for this book. It is the result of many people who have contributed, encouraged, lived, shared, and inspired the content within these pages.

First, thanks to the many refugees and immigrants I've been privileged to know these last eight years. You have taught me more than you know. You are my heroes in many ways.

I'm indebted to a group of people who inspired me to step out and build my platform. First, Nate Mitchell, who helped me take the first plunge and start a blog. Nate was my "computer guy" who I went to for constant counsel.

Also, Carl Johnson and Joe Wells. You both were instrumental in helping me get my message out. Thank you for inspiring me to blog consistently and use social media to share my voice, and for the design work you did for my website. I would be remiss if I did not mention Rob Goodfellow and Shane Sevo. Thanks for all your help.

To Tim Grissom, my editor, and in many ways, my "writing mentor." Thanks for your tireless labor on my manuscript and helping me see things that I couldn't see.

To Sean Benesh at Urban Loft Publishers. Thanks for taking a chance on me, for your encouragement, and for doing an amazing job with this book. You are incredible!

To Frank Stirk, my copyeditor, who did such a great job in cleaning up my manuscript.

To Carl Johnson for his incredible design work on the book cover. You've got such a gift.

To World Relief Chicago. You are some of the best people in the world, doing amazing work for the Kingdom!

Thanks NAMB (especially Steve Canter) for the many opportunities to write.

Thanks to Andy Gardner at Fairlane Alliance Church, Lewie, and Pete for being such advocates for me. Thanks to the Great Lakes District of the Christian & Missionary Alliance Church, and, especially, to New Faith Chapel.

Thanks to all of my blog readers, and for the many people I've met online who have supported and encouraged me. (Many of you have helped spread the word about this book. Thank you!)

To my family: Mom, George, Dad, Katie, Dan, Frank, Kellie, Sandy and Al, Papa, and Grandma Ruby who told me she prays for my book every night. Thanks for your love and support.

And most importantly, to my wife, Angie. Without your support and encouragement none of this would have happened. You believed in me even when I didn't. Also to my son, Luke, who gives me more inspiration and joy each day then he even realizes. You both are the love of my life!

Finally, this wouldn't be possible without the undeserved love and grace of my Lord and Savior. I've felt displaced most of my life. But God has always given me a place in His family. I long for the day when I can see Him and to say, as Paul, "then I shall know fully, even as I am fully known" (1 Corinthians 13:12).

Urban Loft Publishers

Urban Loft Publishers focuses on ideas, topics, themes, and conversations about all-things urban. The city is the central theme and focus of the materials we publish. Given our world's rapid urbanization and dense globalization comes the need to continue to hammer out a theology of the city, as well as the impetus to adapt and model urban ministry to the changing twenty-first century city. It is our intention to continue to mix together urban ministry, theology, urban planning, architecture, transportation planning, and the social sciences as we push the conversation forward about renewing the city. While we lean heavily in favor of scholarly and academic works, we also explore the fun and lighter side of cities as well. Welcome to the new urban world.

www.theurbanloft.org
Portland, Oregon

Other Books by Urban Loft Publishers

The Mission Church Fieldbook by **Leonard Hjalmarson**

Tools for helping believers transition into missional practices have been absent or rare: until now. *The Fieldbook* is a tool for use in groups to transition from inward to outward focus, and to work together to discover shared disciplines of mission and community. *The Fieldbook* will require that you ... move from the life of a member to a missionary ... begin a journey to an unknown destination ... open your life deeply to at least three other people ... recognize that you are God's possession and inheritance ... reimagine your life within God's big story ... discover a messy spirituality ... get outside your comfort zone.

"This is a practical guidebook to help churches and adventuresome folk actually implement a communal way of life on mission that is both transformative and sustainable. By casting the themes within a simple 7-day rhythm, groups are able to readily assimilate perspectives and practices conducive to Jesus apprenticeship. I highly recommend it as a tool for mobilizing the people of God."

Dan Steigerwald, DMin
North America Director,
Christian Associates International

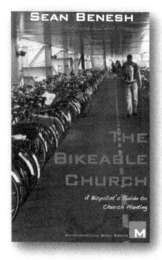

***The Bikeable Church: A Bicyclist's Guide to Church Planting* by Sean Benesh**

The Bikeable Church: A Bicyclist's Guide to Church Planting is an off-the-cuff look and exploration into the bicycling world in Portland. More than that, it pokes and prods church planting in the urban petri dish to discover what it'd be like to plant pedal-powered churches. Chalked full of stories, antics, and slightly questionable research, *The Bikeable Church* spins forward the church planting revolution in light of the changing transportation infrastructure in cities like Portland, and asks whether we can truly start churches where the primary vehicle of use is the bicycle. This book is for the everyday bicyclist and ordinary church planter. You'll be happy to hear that no spandex was worn for the writing of this book.

"To be missional is to be culturally aware. To be missional is to be a strategic thinker. To be missional is to see social diversity. To be missional is to be alert to socio-cultural shifts. To be missional is to live into the mission of God. To be missional is to be "His ambassadors" of reconciliation and restoration of humanity with God. To be missional is to live "Christ" in contemporary time-context. To be missional is to look the mission of Christ through fresh eyes at the cultural shifts. Sean Benesh gets it! The Bikeable Church is more than primmer on church planting to a particular demographic. In clear, concise terms Sean communicates what it means to be a missional theologian. This is an insightful read igniting missional wisdom for our time and context."

Roger Trautmann, DMin
Associate Professor of Pastoral Ministry,
Director of Mentored Ministry Formation,
Multnomah Biblical Seminary/Multnomah University
Portland, Oregon